THE GREEN BERET GUIDE FOR SUCCESS

THE STRATEGIES OF THE QUIET PROFESSIONALS

BOB MAYER

THE GREEN BERET
GUIDE FOR SUCCESS

The Strategies of the Quiet Professionals

By BOB MAYER

INTRODUCTION

Why Should You Read This Book?

In tough times, it's the tough who succeed. The first thing you'll sense when you meet a Green Beret is that they exude *confidence*. It's a palpable sensation. They have confidence in themselves, their team, their unit and Special Forces. However, they rarely boast or make their accomplishments public, thus gaining the moniker the 'Quiet Professionals' over the decades. They just get the job done.

How did they become this way?

They followed a path blazed before them by others, were willing to learn, do hard things and, most importantly, change. That's what this is all about. You wouldn't have picked this book up if there wasn't something in your life you wanted to change. It could be a minor thing or it could be life-altering. This book will illuminate the path to change.

By reading this book you will gain the insight and knowledge to change the same way Special Forces soldiers transition from regular soldiers to being the best. This book gives you a comprehensive plan to build self-confidence.

The definition of confidence is: Trust in a person or thing. A feeling of assurance.

You have goals in your life. You want to achieve things. For most, the largest obstacle to success is fear. This book brings templates and tactics used by the US Army's Green Berets to conquer fear, build confidence and succeed.

What you want to succeed at is personal, varying from reader to reader. In addition to the tools, you'll find examples for using them in a variety of situations. You'll learn how to customize these templates to fit your goals.

This is a complete program for life, covering a broad spectrum from goal setting, to characters to leadership, communication, training and, finally, utilization. They all connect with you at the very center. The tools work both for the individual and for organizations.

But before you start, you have to ask yourself one very important question:

Do You Want To Change?

It's that simple. Change is extremely difficult, for many different reasons, which will be covered in this book. The good news is, experts have blazed the way for you and you can use their lessons learned and the techniques they developed.

A successful person can make decisions and take action in the face of fear. The successful are head and shoulders above their peers and competition. They accomplish their goals, have pride in themselves, and find a way to achieve what they want in life. The successful dare to take chances and succeed.

Fear is the number one barrier that keeps you rooted in the mundane and ordinary. It is the primary obstacle to achieving your dreams. Successful people take action despite their fears. As you'll discover, it is not a question of ignoring fear, but rather the opposite: you must factor fear into your life and deal with it.

A lot of what you will learn in this book seems common sense. Some will also be counter-intuitive. We make repeated mistakes in our lives without learning from them. This book teaches how to focus, learn from errors, and not repeat them. Since we all make mistakes, the positive news is that correspondingly there are ways we can improve. We are emotional creatures, and often our emotions over-rule our common sense. Intellectually, our subconscious often over-powers our conscious. We will focus on trying to find the real reasons why we do things, which are often right in front of us, but we are blind to.

The book is broken down into three areas. In each are three tools, each simplified to one word.

The first tool we'll work with is **WINS**. Why? Because it's key to know where you're going—what you want to change to (goals)—first. You have to understand **What** you want to change; **Why** you want to change; and **Where** the change will occur.

From there we will go to **WHO**. Why? Because once you know what you want to Win, you need to understand yourself. You have to understand what your **Character** can do, what it can't do (yet) and what your blind spot is; what is **Change** and how do you do it; and how to build **Courage** to change.

Finally, we will tackle **DARES**. Why? Because once you know what you want to Win, and understand Who your are, it's time to take risks and push yourself from ordinary to

successful. You have to **Communicate** effectively to implement your change among others; take **Command** of your
change; and then **Complete** the Circle of Success, pulling
all nine tools together to Conquer Fear and Succeed.

How Does The Green Beret Guide Work?

Most books about personal improvement take either a
scientific, practical approach, or a nebulous, theoretical
angle. In *The Green Beret Guide* I combine two apparently
unrelated approaches: the practical way Special Forces
personnel train and operate, and the creativity of an artist's
process.

This book is focused on the individual, but successful
people are the building blocks of successful teams. So once
the individual Circle of Success is completed, a *team* Circle
of Success can be implemented (Appendix E). Special
Forces develops the world's most effective warriors and
builds them into the most flexible and elite fighting unit on
Earth: the Special Forces A-Team. This book is the first step
in building the winning A-Team. As we get further into the
book, I discuss teams more and more because we are all
parts of teams—whether they be family, social or work
related.

Special Operations Forces soldiers are the military's
artists: those who have honed their craft so well, they can
create and achieve beyond that which is the norm.

In Appendix C, Immediate Action Drills are designed
exactly as the words indicate: to allow immediate responses
to problems. They are succinct summaries of concepts and
actions to be taken for each tool. In Appendix D, I show you
the tools applied as I wrote this book.

Here's what you'll see in every tool:

- Introduction—an over-view of the tool.
- A Blood Lesson example to highlight the importance of the tool.
- A step-by-step description breaking the tool down into usable templates.
- Challenges, to help you implement the templates in your life.
- An *Artist's Imagination* example of how the tool works in the creative world of writing.

What Are Blood Lessons?

I use blood lessons as teaching tools, the same way the US Army Special Forces, the Green Berets, do. These are the most successful, flexible fighting soldiers in the world. Their list of successes is long. Person for person, they have earned more military awards, won more battles, and influenced our nation's foreign policy far more than any other military organization. But sometimes it's the lessons learned from failures that are the most touching and enlightening.

What most people don't realize is that the Green Berets achieve as much, if not more, in peacetime, as they do during war. They are not Rambos—they're teachers. This book is your personal window into their (and other special operator's) world, and how they achieve what they do. Learn from them, and apply what you learn to your world.

I use historical examples, because blood lessons are poignant. At times they might seem so much larger than day-to-day life, but I've picked dramatic examples so that they stay with you.

The tactics, theories, and practices in this book were not developed on Wall Street, invented by a think tank, imagined in a university ivory tower, hammered out at the club over cocktails, or theorized in a corporate boardroom. They were forged in blood across the spectrum of time, on battlefields around the world.

What Is The Circle of Success?

The nine *Green Beret Guide* tools form a Circle of Success. Each tool connects with the others at the center, where you stand: creating a clear path to follow to accomplish your life goals. When you reach the last tool in this book, you circle right back to the first, and you'll find that your answers to the exercises you've already completed have changed based on what you've learned on your path. You stand at the center of the Circle as the linchpin that connects all the tools.

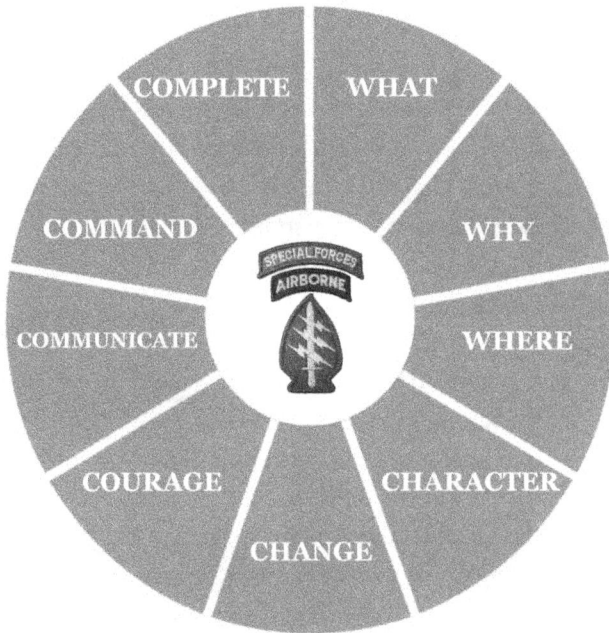

How Are You Feeling So Far?

Take a deep breath.

For those of you worried this is going to be a hard-core, do-or-die, military book, where you'll be doing push-ups in the rain, relax. I'm combining the *Warrior's Spirit* with the *Artist's Imagination*, because I've been both in my life and have found a way to mesh them into a unique path that I invite you to journey with me.

I took Green Beret concepts, ventured into the creative world of fiction writing, and have published over eighty books. I even co-write with romantic suspense writer Jenny Crusie. Our novels seem far away from, as Jenny puts it: "A grim, paranoid, Green Beret thriller writer" collaborating with a romantic comedy writer. But it worked well enough, that our books consistently hit the NY Times, Wall Street Journal, and Publishers Weekly Bestsellers lists, among others. If these tools could work for me in this dynamic situation, it can work for you, no matter your particular path.

I've made the process as simple as possible, but I do warn you that simple doesn't mean easy. As you will see in Tool Five—Change—just reading this book isn't going to be enough. *The Green Beret Guide* is full of moments of enlightenment, the first of the three steps of change. But change is about more than moments.

Your decisions to change and then commit to sustained actions will begin a difficult, but rewarding path. A successful circle you'll build on for the rest of your life.

Green Berets thrive on challenges. They're triple volunteers: Volunteering for the Army, volunteering to become Airborne Qualified, and volunteering for Special Forces training. No one makes them volunteer. No one is going to make you do anything in this book. It's your challenge. This book will help you take your challenge, change, and succeed.

The key to taking the challenge is to face your fear.

Fear drives most of our lives and keeps us from living to the fullest of our potential. It is the most difficult thing we have to deal with and the most necessary thing to overcome in order to change and be successful. You can't ignore fear, suppress it, or let it debilitate you. You must face it, factor it into your life, and then conquer it using the tools you'll gain from reading this book.

What Do You Fear?

As you read this book, you'll be challenged to examine your life:

What wakes you in the middle of the night and causes you to stare out into the darkness with a gnawing feeling deep inside?

What task do you put off and avoid doing as long as possible?

What is the one thing in your life you least *want* to do, but know you *should* do?

What is the one thing in your life you most want to do, but have been afraid to try?

Which people do you least want to interact with, but know you should?

Which decision do you know you should make and implement, but lack the personal leadership to make the commitment to do?

What course of action would you like to pursue, but you fear people around you will disapprove or even actively try to stop you from doing?

Take the Challenge: Exercise 1
Write down the one thing you fear the most.
(The fear in your head is not in the real world. Writing down your fear externalizes it, so you can take action to conquer it in the real world).

(The fear in your head is not in the real world. Writing down your fear externalizes it, so you can take action to conquer it in the real world).

It's not by chance that the three major areas are Who, Dares and Wins. Who Dares Wins is the motto of the British Special Air Service, Britain's elite Special Operations Force, and nine other elite special operations forces around the world, so there must be something to it that the members of these units like. The US Special Forces and Delta Force base much of their operational templates, training, and Assessment & Selection of personnel, on the lessons learned by the British Special Air Service.

To succeed beyond the norm, you have to be daring. Take risks. When you do, using the proper preparation and the tools illustrated in this book, you will change and succeed.

What's Your Primary Motivator?

To be successful at facing fear, you have to understand what motivates you. Understanding this is just as important as understanding your reaction to fear.

What keeps you going, even when everything seems to be going wrong?

What pushes back the darkness in your life and makes you feel positive?

What thought and feeling do you draw on in order to do tasks you dread doing?

What is the ONE thing you would fight to the death to defend?

What person do you most respect and why?

Take the Challenge: Exercise 2
Write down the one thing that motivates you the most.

Look at the conflict between your fear in exercise 1 and motivation in exercise 2. That conflict can make success a struggle. A battle. Except your primary enemy is inside you.

If you spend your life battling yourself, wasting energy that could be used to make your reality better, the majority of your time will be spent reacting to your fears and nightmares, not working toward the success you dream about.

Remember, it takes as much energy to be average as to be successful. It's just a question of where the energy is directed. This book will teach you to take the energy you spend battling yourself, reacting, and being in crisis, and redirect it into positive change and success.

It is said that most truths are paradoxes. *The Green Beret*

Guide is a set of successful techniques, ideas and examples that will take you on your own unique path. However, don't allow anything you read here to stifle *your* creativity. Your dreams are the key to your own personal success.

If you were a painter, *The Green Beret Guide* would be your primer on understanding paint, canvas, lighting and perspective. How to sell your work to a gallery, and so on. But as an artist, you would ultimately be the one who has to decide *what* you want to paint and *how* to paint it.

You are unique. Your life, job, family and situation are unique to you. Most importantly, your goals are unique. The word 'successful' means different things to each person. Adjust the templates to yourself and your goals. And once you've accomplished that, let the creativity that is boiling inside of you flow forth to take you to even higher levels along with those around you. One of the most important strengths of a Special Forces A-Team is the ability to tap into each member's specific area of expertise along with their creativity and knowledge for the benefit of the team and goal accomplishment. We are all members of teams, whether the team is our family, those we work with, our friends, or society as a whole.

You must first master the craft of being successful, as any artist or warrior must master the basics of their particular discipline. But then, allow your brilliance to lead you as you tailor Green Beret techniques to overcoming your fears. Be original. Be a creative force in your own life. That is why at the end of this book I talk about breaking rules and taking risks under Dares.

Green Berets and artists blaze new paths, innovating strategies and tactics as they go. So can you.

. . .

THE GOAL **of this Book**

To introduce you to the core tactical areas of Special Forces so you can succeed in the face of fear. A quick definition below to clear up something that confuses people which is the difference between Special Operations Forces and Special Forces (Green Berets):

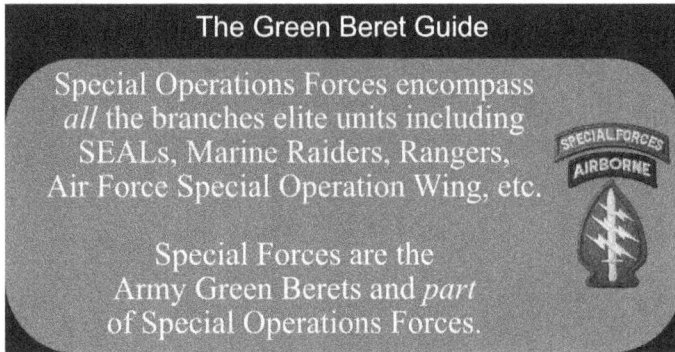

The Green Beret Guide

Special Operations Forces encompass *all* the branches elite units including SEALs, Marine Raiders, Rangers, Air Force Special Operation Wing, etc.

Special Forces are the Army Green Berets and *part* of Special Operations Forces.

Do you want to be ordinary or do you want to be elite?

It's that simple. Ordinary means average. By definition elite are the best or most skilled members of a group.

Which do you want to be?

This is the first test. If you answer: "Ordinary" or "Average," then shut this book and forget about it. But if you enjoy challenges and want to be the best you are capable of, read on.

Do you want to live a life ruled by fear, or do you want to live to the fullest, led by positive emotions?

Do you really want to take the chances—that if you don't take you will regret on your deathbed? Regrets are a terrible thing to have and most people have too many.

An elite person is someone who can make decisions and take action in the face of fear. It is a person who is clearly head and shoulders above his/her peers and competition in terms of goal accomplishment. It is a person who has pride in themselves. It is a person who can do and achieve what they want in life. It is a person who can take chances and succeed.

Fear is the number one obstacle that keeps you rooted in the mundane and ordinary. It is the primary obstacle that keeps you from achieving your dreams. Successful people are those who take action despite their fears. As we will cover later in this book, it is not a question of ignoring fear, but rather the opposite: factoring it in as part of your life and dealing with it. Sometimes it is even using fear as a motivator rather than a debilitating factor.

THE FIVE PERCENT Rule

If everyone were elite, then there would be no elite. I believe the elite are the top five percent. Why did I settle on that that number? Because studies have shown that only five percent of people are capable of internally motivated, sustained change. I will cover this in detail further on when we discuss change under character. Certainly some people are born with unique gifts and talents, but the elite, as we will discuss them in this book, are the people who make a decision to take the road less traveled and stay the course. Thus elite is not a birth-right but something any of us can achieve if we have enough 'grit'.

What is grit?

Science has too long focused on intelligence & talent as determiners of success. And it's not. *The key to success is to set a specific long-term goal and to do whatever it takes until the goal has been achieved.* That's called *GRIT* (defined as courage and resolve; strength of character).

Angele Duckworth, author of *Grit: The Power of Passion*

and Perseverance, studied successful people and also those who passed through the toughest weeding out processes. She wanted to uncover what character traits led to successfully negotiating those tests. Two of the primary ones she studied I have personal experience in: Beast Barracks (plebe summer at West Point) and the Special Forces Qualification Course (the Q Course).

My plebe squad had five members. Three of them didn't make it to Christmas the first year. They weren't bad people; they just didn't really WANT it. It's the same in Special Forces training. There are those who go into it because they want to wear a green beret. They don't make it. The ones who make it want to *BE* a Green Beret. This book is what it takes and how it works.

Note that there is additional material in the Appendixes besides those already mentioned including:

Appendix F: Welcome to the World of Special Operators which gives the history of Special Operations Forces and discusses other units.

Appendix G: The Recent History and Organization of Special Operations Forces.

Appendix H: The Lessons of History. This is in terms of Special Forces.

Appendix I: Leadership Styles. From MacArthur to Patton to Eisenhower, some key military leaders and their varied styles.

These is a lot of repetition in this book. That is on purpose. Not only is it a valid teaching method, the Circle of Success implies repetition as we go around repeatedly, improving each time.

Do You Have A Fixed Mindset Or A Growth Mindset?

Successful people have a growth mindset. The problem with many talented people is that they know they are talented; they believe that they already know everything they need to know. So they never adapt and change and grow. A growth mindset person believes they can always learn more.

One of the most difficult aspects of living a successful life and being elite is that often you must go against the norm and the mass of other people's opinions and expectations about the way you should live. There is a strong power in society trying to pull you into the ninety-five percent of people who live in fear and with mediocrity. This book will show you ways to go against the norm successfully and with minimum external conflict.

The very fact you are reading this book means you have a growth mindset.

For an organization to be elite, first the people inside of it must be elite. Elite individuals and organizations must have excellent goal-setting, leadership, training and communications. As this book progresses we will move from elite individuals to the elements of team building which make elite organizations.

What is the Most Important Asset You Have?

If you answered anything other than yourself, you most definitely need to read on. Your character is the core of your life. The *intent*—a term which we will discuss in more detail under goals—of this book is for you to understand and accept the focus of leadership, communication, training and goal setting that gets unified so that a person and organization can succeed at whatever they desire.

This is the first area in which the *Green Beret Guide*

differs from the norm: People and character are a higher priority than mission/goals. Yet, paradoxically, by making people a higher priority, goal accomplishment is more often achieved.

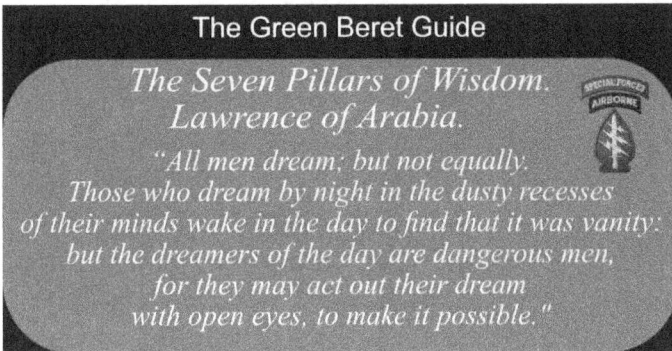

The Green Beret Guide

The Seven Pillars of Wisdom.
Lawrence of Arabia.

"All men dream; but not equally.
Those who dream by night in the dusty recesses
of their minds wake in the day to find that it was vanity;
but the dreamers of the day are dangerous men,
for they may act out their dream
with open eyes, to make it possible."

Be a Day Dreamer

There is a large difference between having a dream and having a nightmare. The latter is when you are consumed by fear. Dreams are the first steps of achievement, but only the first step. As noted earlier, dreams that remain inside your head are not real until you take action and externalize them.

An interesting question to ask yourself is this: If I had financial security and freedom, would I be where I am right now, doing what I'm doing?

If the answer is no, then you are ruled by fear.

If you are in a committed relationship, are you there because you love the other person and care about their growth as a human being, or because you don't want to be alone?

If the answer is the latter, then you are ruled by fear and doing that other person a dis-service.

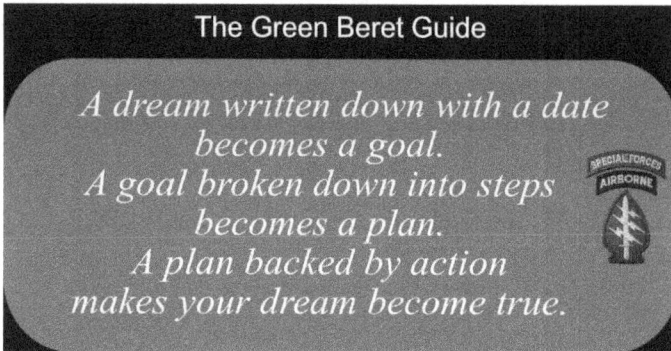

The Green Beret Guide

A dream written down with a date becomes a goal.
A goal broken down into steps becomes a plan.
A plan backed by action makes your dream become true.

In the Green Beret Guide I am combining two apparently diverse approaches: the way Special Forces conduct missions and the way an artist creates. I have found that most books concerning people and organizations take either a scientific, practical approach, or a nebulous, theoretical angle. This book combines artistic theory with practical guides for implementing the theory along with historical examples to learn from. I view Green Berets as the military's artists, those who have honed their craft so well, they can create and achieve beyond that which is the norm.

The format of this book is unusual in that I am mixing fact, theories and, as we get further in, both factual and fictionalized historical incidents to present the information. The latter is used to bring to life lessons learned and make it easier for you to both identify with those who have gone before and to remember what happened. Plus, fact and theories touch the intellect, but the emotional side is actually more important (as we will discuss under character) and the fictionalized historical excerpts are ways to reach that.

I project quite a bit of information at you in this book. I liken reading it to trying to take a drink from a fire hydrant. You'll quench your thirst but there will be a lot coming at you that might not quite fit in place right now. But I make you one guarantee right up front:

You will find at least one thing in this book that you can immediately use to make yourself more successful.

AREA ONE: WINS

The Green Beret Guide

WINS:

Have goals (*What*) that are clearly stated.

Understand *Why* you are trying to those goals.

Analyze and understand the environment

(*Where*) you are trying to achieve those goals.

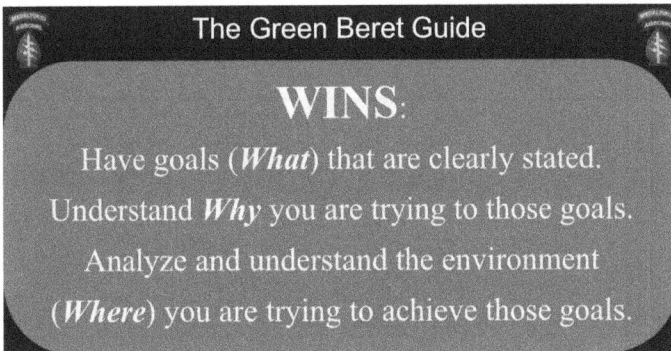

We'll cover Wins first, because it's best to have a clear direction as you work through the next two areas. Using Green Beret techniques in this area, you'll begin by specifying goals, then understanding why you want to achieve them, and finish with studying the situation in which you are trying to have success.

We will work on WHAT (goals) you want to change. Then examine WHY (intent) you want to change and achieve your goals. Then study WHERE (environment) change will occur.

Goals are future oriented. Planning for the future is a cornerstone of Special Forces. A successful individual acts, while the norm is trying to maintain the status quo with your environment. Most people do not have well-defined, clear goals and thus never change. They spend significant time in their lives reacting, instead of acting. Trying to achieve a goal through reaction is a self-defeating approach: you're allowing your efforts to be dictated by external forces and other's goals. To avoid this, it's important that you apply the three tools in this area to your life, then you'll be on the path to succeed.

TOOL ONE: HAVE GOALS (WHAT)
THAT ARE CLEARLY STATED

The One Sentence Goal Statement

The *one sentence goal* is the tool that will become the foundation of everything you do, from day to day goals to life changing ones. Having an idea of where you're going, before you start on your path, is a key tenet of Green Beret operations. Then, being aware of the priority of goals and aligning the hierarchy can reduce conflict and enhance success.

Clearly understanding your goals, keeps you on target to succeed.

> ┌─────────────────────────────────┐
> │ The Green Beret Guide   │
> │   │
> │ **Special Forces Assessment** │
> │ **and Selection Thought:**   │
> │ *Take your eyes off the price and* │
> │ *put them on the prize.*   │
> └─────────────────────────────────┘

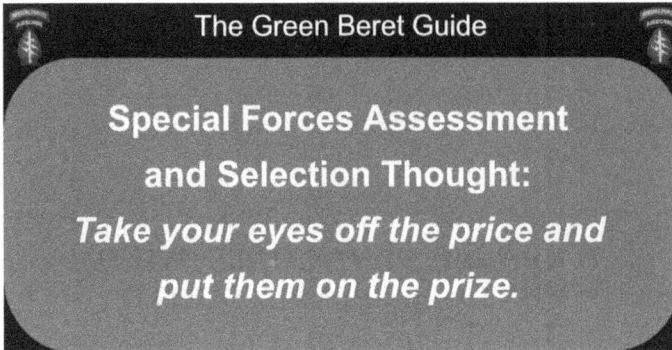

Blood Lesson: The Man Who Never Was

Let's look at a *What* for a complex large Special Operations problem that was successfully solved, beginning with a one-sentence goal.

The Problem

In 1943, the Allies were poised to invade Europe after successfully invading North Africa. The next obvious place to attack was Sicily. To quote Churchill, "Anyone but a fool would realize it's Sicily."

There was a very big problem: *How to stop the Germans from massing their forces in Sicily and defeating the invasion?*

Solving this problem was tasked to an officer in MI-5, the forerunner of the British Special Operations Executive (SOE). Lieutenant Commander Montagu decided the British needed to give the Germans solid evidence that the attack would occur elsewhere. Evidence that they would believe.

He boiled this complex problem down to this one sentence WHAT:

I will implement a plan to convince the Germans the attack is coming some place other than Sicily far enough before the actual invasion to influence the German reaction.

The Solution

This simple, one-sentence '*What* do I want to achieve?' led to a very complex plan to solve the problem:

Montagu found a corpse: a homeless man who had died of pneumonia. During an autopsy, such a death would appear very similar to that of a person who'd drowned.

He created a military persona for the man. A complete identity, down to the smallest detail. The homeless corpse became Captain/Acting Major William Martin, Royal Marine.

Montagu went so far as to place theater stubs in 'Martin's' pockets along with love letters from his 'fiancée', a clerk in Montagu's office. In a briefcase chained to 'Major Martin's' body, certain key documents were placed, all fakes: letters between generals discussing a dual attack on Sardinia/Corsica and one against Greece. The letters said a deception plan was being implemented to fool the Germans into thinking the attack would really take place against Sicily.

The body, packed in ice, was put in a canister, placed aboard a British submarine, and sailed to a point off the Spanish Coast. The submarine surfaced, the body was unpacked, a life jacket was placed around it, and it was cast into the ocean. The body was found by a Spanish fisherman the next day and the documents eventually wound up in the hands of German agents. It was turned over the British consulate a few days later. Sans briefcase. The British demanded the return of the documents and the Spanish government complied. Examining them, the British discovered that they had been surreptitiously opened. The fake evidence had been read by the Germans.

With what results?

Hitler was so convinced of the truth of the documents

that he ignored the common and logical belief that Sicily was the site of the next Allied attack. The Germans deployed forces to both Sardinia/Corsica and Greece. They also redeployed two Panzer divisions from the Russian front to Greece under the command of Field Marshall Rommel, weakening themselves in an area even Montagu couldn't have anticipated.

The Lesson

Montagu's clear understanding of the What of his mission paid off in dividends that changed the course of World War II even beyond the invasion of Sicily. During the invasion of Normandy, when the Germans captured *real* top secret documents from an abandoned landing craft showing future Allied operations, Hitler refused to believe them, feeling they were another set-up, even though they were real.

All this, from one simple *What*.

State Your Goals in One Sentence

Here's what you're looking for in your sentence:

- Positive verb: the action that you want to achieve.
- A verb that indicates an action you control.
- Concise, understandable wording.
- An external, visible, outcome to achieve.
- A time lock for accomplishing the goal if applicable.

Keep it positive. A negative goal accepts defeat.

A boxer with a goal to "Not to get my head beaten off," is already down for the count. If you want to lose weight, avoid saying "I don't want to be over-weight." Where's the action?

Perhaps what you mean instead is, "I want to work out for a minimum of thirty minutes each day to be physically fit." Then add a second goal: "Every day, I will carefully watch what I eat to only consume healthy foods."

Don't define your goals in terms of whatever crisis you fear coming toward you. We'll plan for possible catastrophes later. It's enough for now to figure out a positive, understandable, external *What*. This clearly defined goal will keep you on your Circle of Success path when you're enmeshed in working with the other eight tools.

Most people spend their lives in crisis, overly-focused on obstacles and fears, with no clear goal in mind. Thus, they never change. A successful person must rise above crisis mode and continue to move toward his or her goals. When they do that, they begin to change.

In Special Forces, the mission statement drives everything else. The mission statement is the Green Beret's *What*. Each team is assigned specific goals. Each person on the team is also assigned specific goals that, when achieved, lead to mission success.

Many people view their lives as a series of complex problems that require complex solutions and they quickly become overwhelmed. But what if they narrowed their goals down to a simple, attainable series of *What* sentences?

> ### The Green Beret Guide
>
> *A dream written down with a date
> becomes a goal.
> A goal broken down into steps
> becomes a plan.
> A plan backed by action
> makes your dream become true.*

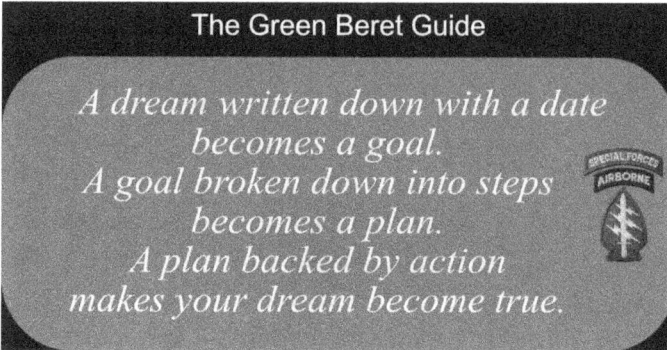

To define your goals, you need to ask yourself several key questions:

What do you fear doing? Our greatest inhibitor from achieving our goals is usually a blind spot. Successful people walk directly into what they fear the most and conquer it.

Why did other people do it?

How will you know when you have achieved your goal?

What will be the external, visible result?

How did others define it?

Did anyone else want to achieve this goal? It is most likely you won't be the first person to attempt this.

How long did it take other people to do this? What is the time lock for achieving this goal?

When you write down your goals, make sure every word means something. Test it by showing it to others who you respect and have them give it back to you in their own words.

You will have a great degree of latitude in deciding *how* you want to achieve a goal after you have written it down, but the first step is making sure you have the goal. It is much the same way an author has to write down the original idea that started their creative process and then come up with story. Every idea has been done, and pretty much every goal has been also; the difference comes in the follow-up. That is where your creativity comes in.

Sometimes your goal can be a *way* to do something, rather than the something itself.

Your goal can't change– all else can– thus allowing innovation off of a solid base. If you change your goal, everything else has to change. You have chosen a different path.

A simple example among the Green Berets using these questions:

The goal: A Special Forces candidate will complete the twelve-mile forced march with 55 pounds worth of equipment in under three hours.

Why should anyone else want to achieve this goal? It's been a standard for years. And there is a reason for the standard, as Special Forces soldiers spend a great deal of time making long overland movements with much heavier loads than this. The only person I ever had removed from my A-Team was because he could not keep up on our overland movements under heavy loads.

What do you fear doing? Leading up to this 12-mile march, candidates are tested doing various distances where the time standard is *not* told them. This forces them to make decisions that could determine whether or not they succeed, going directly at their greatest fear of failing the course.

Why did other people do it? Throughout history, soldiers have ultimately had to rely on their feet to get them where they're going. Even in modern warfare, 'boots on the ground' still make the final difference.

How will you know when you have achieved your goal? What will be the external, visible result? You'll have completed the march in under three hours.

How did others define it? 12 miles, three hours, varied terrain, is the standard for the Expert Infantry Badge.

For example, for the goal above, the Candidate has a goal of completing the twelve-mile rucksack march under three hours. That is subordinate to the goal of successfully passing the Special Forces Qualification Course. But that is subordinate to a primary goal of becoming a Special Forces Soldier. Everything that candidate does is based on the primary goal.

Take the Challenge: Exercise 3
In one sentence, write down a short-term goal that you want to achieve in the next seven days.

Does the sentence makes sense? Does each word mean something? Is the verb a positive action? Is there an external, visible outcome so you can judge whether you've achieved you goal? Do you have a time lock to achieve it within the next week?

Remember, Montagu's *What* wasn't, "Stop the Germans from believing the invasion would come in Sicily." His positive goal led him to take an action, and his solution *made* the Germans think something else.

. . .

ORGANIZATION GOALS

If you are searching for your organization's primary goal, here is a way to figure it out: Why was this organization founded? What was the original goal? I think the primary goal is almost always the original goal unless something drastic has happened, in which case, even if it has the same name, it is no longer the same organization, and somewhere along the way it was 're-founded'.

For organizations ask the following questions:

- Your organization was founded for?
- The most important division of your company is?
- Your primary product is?
- Your brand is?
- How do you know when your goal has been accomplished?

Just as in writing a novel, the most important person to consider is the reader, for an organization, the most important person to consider is the customer/consumer.

HIERARCHY OF GOALS

- Organizational Goal (Strategic)
- Subordinate Unit Goal (Tactical)
- Specific Mission Goal
- Individual Goal
- For Organization (job)
- For Mission (task)

HERE IS a Special Forces **organizational goal:**

- Special Forces will be prepared to conduct the six SOF missions of Unconventional Warfare, Direct Action, Special Reconnaissance, Foreign Internal Defense, Counter-terrorism, and Coalition Warfare/Support.

Here is an A-Team's **subordinate unit goal:**

- ODA 055 will be prepared to conduct all SOF missions with an emphasis on Strategic Reconnaissance with maritime operations capability.

Here is a **mission goal:**

- ODA 055 will infiltrate Operational Area Claw to conduct Strategic Reconnaissance along the designated sector of rail line for fourteen days reporting movement of battalion level and higher units.

Note as we get down to tactical goals, a time factor comes into play.

Here are the two types of **individual goals:**

- Senior Communications Sergeant will maintain a secure link with higher headquarters. (organization/job)
- Senior Communications Sergeant will report all designated traffic battalion level or higher along

rail line to higher headquarters four times daily. (mission/task)

Note that all these goals are in alignment. Conflict occurs when goals do not align.

Align The Hierarchy Of Goals In The Same Direction

In an organization, a leader's responsibility is to make people realize the unit's goal is in line with their individual goal. That a convergence of the two will benefit all. It is more important for the leaders to realize this than the followers.

Make sure that your goals align or else much energy will be wasted in the conflict inherent in failing to do so. If your goal is to lose weight, then your eating habits and your physical activities both have to support that goal. This sounds simple and basic but you would be amazed at how often people defeat themselves and keep themselves from achieving their goals. While we prefer to rail against the world and 'them', the enemy is most often ourselves.

The primary goal, based on your 'one thing' cannot change. Because everything in your life is built on it. However, I have found in the process of creating, that the original vision tends to get lost to a certain extent. It is the same when writing a novel. I am a big believer in writing down goals and posting them where I can see them every day, so that I don't forget and stay on the same path every day.

A peacetime example of a lack of goal setting: When I was a team leader, the battalion operations officer called me in to his office. He told me he wanted my team to set up a combination land navigation course/ rifle range. He said the commander wanted the men to go through a strenuous overland movement and finish at the rifle range where they would qualify on their weapons.

I asked the operations officer what the primary objective of the exercise was. Was it to qualify on weapons? Or to practice land navigation? You can only have one primary goal. His response was that the battalion commander, our boss, wanted the men to go through a 'gut check'. Which was neither of the above.

Problem number one: I was told to do three things. While all could be part of one exercise, what I really needed to know, and what I hadn't been told, was the *primary* objective of the training I was to plan. While this might not seem an issue initially—after all it appears all I had to do was set up a land navigation course ending at a rifle range where the men shot; as you will soon see it became a major problem.

At the same time I was in the operations officer's office, my team sergeant was sitting with the operations sergeant major getting the same—but slightly different—instructions. Which was another problem, indicating the operations office was also confused and passing on different interpretations of the same mission.

I went back to my team room and did a rather strange thing. I pulled out the army field manual for conducting training, blew the dust off of it, and read the chapters on how to plan training. I made some notes, went back to the battalion operations officer, and told him according to the field manual, the primary objective of training needed to be specified before planning could proceed.

Was I greeted with open arms and enthusiasm and a hearty slap on the back for following approved Army procedure?

As you can guess, of course not. After some choice words ending with "You're just a captain and you do what the battalion commander wants!" I was tossed out of the office.

Some of my questions were:

- Was the land navigation important? Or was the goal of the land navigation simply to make the men cover a certain amount of distance before arriving at the firing range, so that they would fire under simulated combat conditions? If so, then I could accomplish the same thing in a much more straight-forward manner by simply having the men do a forced march to the rifle range and save time and effort all around.
- Was this to be our required annual qualification? If so, then the firing was pre-eminent as this was something each soldier had to pass. If so, then a forced march would be detrimental, but a relatively easy land navigation course would not be a problem.
- Was the cross-country movement to be done tactically? Would the men carry full rucksacks?
- What exactly was meant by 'gut check?'

Do you see the number of questions that evolve when the primary objective isn't made clear to those tasked with carrying out the mission? Do you see how many different ways I could have accomplished this vague guidance, with the odds being I was not accomplishing what the commander envisioned?

Eventually word of this reached the Commander. He stopped by my team room and asked me what the problem was. I explained that I could plan and conduct this training, but it would be helpful if I knew what his primary goal was. He explained that his goal was: "I want the men pushed to their limits within the designated time period, both mentally and physically, to test team cohesion."

To me this guidance was very different from running a land navigation course and a rifle range. That was something the operations officer had generated on their own, in their interpretation of the Battalion Commander's vision. Because nothing had been written done and solidified (something we'll discuss under communication), there was dissonance.

What we ended up with was an exercise that we called the Gut Check. We started with a no-notice alert bringing the team in; having them pack up and load out to the airfield; rig for jumping; board an aircraft and conduct a parachute infiltration; they were met on the drop zone by an agent who gave them coordinates for their next point. If they made the next point in time they found food and directions; if they didn't make it in time they found just the directions to the next point. And so on until the team covered an extensive amount of ground in a specified time period. Few teams made it through the gut check successfully and we found it tested team cohesion extremely well as the Battalion Commander had desired. It also forced teams to be completely prepared for no-notice alerts and load outs as they had to take their gear as it was packed in their team room. This stood us in good stead down the line when we received real-world alerts.

The rifle range portion was dropped for logistics reasons. It was something the operations officer had tagged on as something he thought would be a nice addition, but in reality would have forced the planning to go in entirely another direction. I was able to give the commander exactly what he wanted with just one sentence of instructions detailing his intent—something we will discuss shortly.

As you can see from this one example all the elements of the elite were involved: leadership, communication, training, goal-setting and character.

WHAT: The Artist's Imagination

I spend the entire first day of my Writers Workshop having students write a single sentence: the *What* for their book. Being able to say what their book is about in that one sentence helps them focus their book idea. I have found in my study of the creative writing process, that the original vision (WHAT) for a story often gets lost while a novel is being written. Likewise, you can also lose sight of what drives you when you try to change and achieve goals. I spend a large amount of time at the beginning of my Green Beret Guide workshops having people write down their Whats (goals) and analyzing them to make sure they are truly the goals each person wants.

An author has to write down the original idea that starts his creative process before he can come up with story. Every creative idea has been written about before, and pretty much every goal has been tried. The difference in your life will be how you follow up on your goals. That's where your creativity will thrive. That's where your positive emotional energy will drive you.

Write down your goals and post them where you can see them every day, so that you stay on the same path. For a book, I tell writers to post their one-sentence original idea (WHAT) where they see it every day when they begin writing. As with any other goal, it's the one part of the book that can't change without forcing everything else in the Circle of

Success to change. It keeps the author focused, allowing the big picture to be clearly seen in one sentence. It's easy to get lost in the forest amongst the trees in a 400 pages manuscript. Beyond the writing of the book, like Montagu's WHAT serving purposes beyond the immediate one, the one-sentence WHAT for a book is often the core of the pitch to sell the book, from author, to agent, to editor, to publisher, to the sales force, to the bookstore buyer, to the reader.

Take the Challenge: Exercise 4
Divide a piece of lined paper into four equal columns.
Label each column: What, Why, Where, Done.
Under the first column, WHAT, write a subordinate goal
for each of the areas that are applicable to you in which
you want to achieve a goal in the next week (nothing
major, just a basic, simple goal).

TOOL TWO: UNDERSTAND WHY YOU ARE TRYING TO ACHIEVE THOSE GOALS

Understanding *why* you want to change and achieve your goals improves your morale and motivation. It allows you to utilize your initiative and expertise to achieve and succeed. Sometimes, understanding *why* you want to achieve something will change the *what* as you saw in the example in the previous tool.

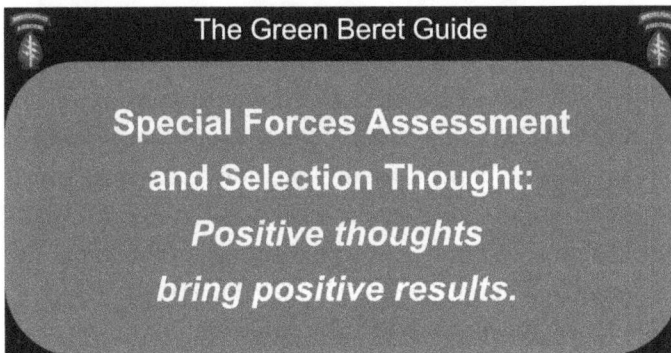

Why Are You Trying To Achieve This Goal?

Concurrent with every goal is intent. The intent is the reason why you are trying to achieve your goal. The goal is usually a *what* statement and factual, while the intent is a *why* statement and psychological. As a novelist it took me ten years of writing and fifteen manuscripts to realize the importance of having an intent to my stories, beyond simply being entertaining. Any time you develop a goal, you are concurrently establishing intent. However, for many people and organizations, the intent remains buried in their subconscious mind and does the organization and person little good. I believe it is critical to not only have that intent in my conscious mind but to write it down to make it real.

The goal is intellectual while the intent is the emotion. And remember, which of the two is more powerful? Intent is where fear starts entering the situation, which we will discuss shortly. Intent takes into account the effect of an action.

The intent and goal should be mutually supportive. Like the goal, the intent should be a positive statement.

A way to state intent is: We are doing X (goal) for this reason Y (intent).

Telling someone what to do but not telling them why they are doing it, is counter-productive and also stymies the initiative of those who must contribute to mission accomplishment. When I first entered the army, the key portion of the operations order was the Mission Statement which detailed *what* the unit was to accomplish. About five years later, someone came up with the idea of adding the Commander's Intent to the Mission Statement. This was adding the *why* behind the what and considerably improved the effectiveness of an operations order.

Like the goal, the intent should be stated positively as people respond better to positive emotions than negative.

Examples of bad intents are:

- Because the boss said so.
- So we don't get fired.
- Because we have nothing better to do.
- So we look busy.

Examples of good intents include:

- -Because it saves me time.
- -So I can do my job more efficiently.
- -Because I will be physically fit and feel better, emotionally and physically.
- -Because it will reduce my anxiety over money and allow me to focus that energy on other things.
- -Because it will improve my relationship with my spouse.
- -Because it *is* fun.
- -Because it is a dream I've always wanted to achieve.

Because intent gives direction but not specific instructions, it allows a large degree of latitude as you further develop your goals and decide how you are going to achieve them. Intent helps you innovate and motivate. Intent is a critical element of Special Forces operations planning because it allows these highly trained soldiers to use their skills and creativity to maximum effect.

Blood Lesson: The Best Defense is to Take Action

The first American Special Operations Force was Rogers' Rangers. Robert Rogers was a colonial farmer from New Hampshire, recruited by the British in 1755 to serve in the

French and Indian War. Over the course of the following years he formed a unit of colonials called Rogers' Rangers, the first Ranger unit.

Unlike the Redcoat British, they wore green uniforms and utilized unconventional tactics, many of which were written down as Rogers' Ranging Rules, some of which are still used in the current US Army Ranger Handbook.

The Problem

The most significant engagement the Rangers fought was with the Abenaki Indians in Canada. This tribe had been raiding the colonies and was credited during the war with over five hundred kills, mostly of civilians.

Rogers' assigned What was, 'Stop the Abenaki.'

Notice this was phrased in the negative and it was a reaction. Rogers saw the problem with that goal.

Conventional wisdom at the time dictated being on the defensive along the frontier. Rogers realized that would leave the initiative in the hands of his enemies.

The Solution

Rogers asked himself *why* they needed to stop the Abenaki: to halt the raids and the killings. Rogers knew the frontier was simply too large to be adequately defended with the scant forces he had. Looking at his *why* changed his *what*.

He decided that the only way to stop the scourge was to go to the source. Change from applying conventional tactics to unconventional ones. Others told him that was impossible—requiring his Rangers to venture too far inside enemy territory and leaving the frontier undefended (taking too great a risk—being too daring).

He changed the reactive, "fearful," *What* verb into a positive action:

I will lead my Rangers to attack and destroy the Abenaki.

His reasoning? If no one considered the raid a real possibility, the enemy wouldn't be prepared to defend against it. It was a risk worth taking.

A successful individual finds new ways to tackle problems, and is willing to take risks to succeed. He is willing to change the status quo.

The Lesson

Leading a Ranger force of two hundred men, he marched into Canada and destroyed the Abenaki village, a feat shown in the 1940 movie *Northwest Passage* starring Spencer Tracy. This was a case of thinking outside of the normal parameters on Rogers' part.

But How Do You Innovate?

Try the following processes:

1. Ask yourself: *What if?* Project out courses of actions, much like a chess master, trying to see how they will play out. Enlist the aid of others in doing this. Particularly focus on suggestions that you have a strong initial negative reaction to. Our greatest weakness have our greatest emotional defenses built around them and that extends to What and Why.

2. Study and research. You are not the first one to face whatever challenge it is that's ahead of you. Study how others did it. We'll discuss this more in the next tool when we cover the Special Forces Area Study.

3. Take it one step further. Yes, maybe you can achieve your goal by doing A. But what about if you go beyond A? What if what appears to be isn't what it appears to be?

4. Reverse your thinking. Stop beating your head against the wall. Back off, and walk around the wall and look at it from the other side. Change your perspective and stop having tunnel vision.

5. What if you're wrong? What if your blind spot is controlling you (something we'll cover in Tool 4, Character)? Sometimes, if things don't feel right, you need to stop and pay attention to those feelings. As a writer, I'm not a big fan of the concept of writer's block—I usually call it laziness. However, if for several days in a row I'm disquieted about what I'm writing, I take that as a warning that I'm going in the wrong direction. At times like that I put the brakes on and step back from what I'm working on. Drop my preconceived notions.

6. Keep it simple. This seems to contradict some of the earlier techniques such as take it one step further. However, when you are doing something completely new to you, it is often best to keep things as simple as possible so that you can focus on the goal and not get bogged down in the process.

Design Boundaries Using Your Why

While intent should be stated positively, you have to be clear about your limits as you define each goal and what you want to change. Successful people should not need much external motivation, but they do need boundaries clearly drawn. You can take any change to an unhealthy extreme.

The key to setting limits is to avoid unexpected, and undesired, results. For example, in Ranger School, the instructors were insistent that the students take action immediately.

The WHY (intent) behind this? In an ambush situation

you don't have to time to think—you have to act, and often in a way that is contrary to common sense. The proper reaction to being ambushed is to assault *into* the ambushing force.

One day a group of Ranger School students were being bussed to a training site. When the bus stopped, an instructor jumped on board screaming at the students to get off the bus NOW! The students took action. They kicked out the windows and poured out of the bus. Needless to say they achieved the *What* the instructors were looking for, but not exactly in a way that was appreciated by the chain of command.

If your goal is to become physically fit, you need to know what your limits are, because going too far can be dangerous and you can end up hurting yourself, negating your goal. Pretty much anything taken to an extreme can be dangerous. We'll discuss this more in Tool Four: Character.

Take the Challenge: Exercise 5
Using the four-column sheet from Exercise 4, fill out the second column. Next to each WHAT, list the WHY in the second column. I am doing X (what) for reason Y (why).

Examine your results. Do you have a positive why?

Are some of your why's reactive?

Are some of your why's based on fear?

For each What that has a negative Why, rewrite the Why to be positive—or consider redefining the What or dropping it.

WHY: The Artist's Imagination

After deciding *What* someone wants to write a book about, I then ask them *Why* they want to write about it. What effect do they wish to achieve? The same story told two slightly different ways will have a very different impact.

The *Why* makes the *What* exciting, because it allows for a variety of approaches. Every *What* has been done--every idea has already been told. But every *Why* hasn't. Being able to give the WHY for a book means the author understands the intent he or she wants to transmit to readers. They know what emotion they desire the reader to walk away with.

They also have a better understanding of their own motivation for writing the book. Sometimes, they realize that their What is wrong because it won't achieve their Why. Then they end up adjusting the What so that it is in line with their intent.

One thing I run into constantly with novel writers is a reaction to suggestions about changing the plot. They say "But that's not what happened!" I gently remind them that they invented the story and the characters. They made it happen. They can un-make it. The resistance to this indicated the difficulty we have in using our imagination and letting go off pre-conceived notions.

TOOL THREE: ANALYZE AND UNDERSTAND THE ENVIRONMENT (WHERE) YOU ARE TRYING TO ACHIEVE THOSE GOALS

U nderstanding your environment helps you work in harmony with it and those around you. In this tool, you'll use the Special Forces Area Study to understand your environment's effect on you, and your effect on your environment.

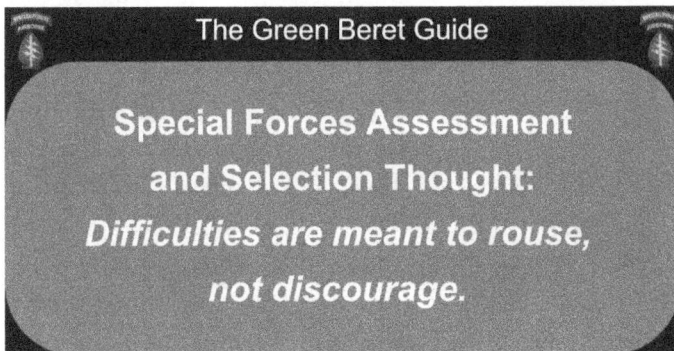

The Green Beret Guide

Special Forces Assessment and Selection Thought:
Difficulties are meant to rouse, not discourage.

Blood Lesson: Learning the Hard Way- The Origin of the SEALs

The Special Forces team I commanded had the additional specialty of being a maritime operations team. We spent a lot of time in the water, including graduating from the Royal Danish Navy's Fromandkorpset (Frogman Corps) Combat Swim school in Denmark. We learned the importance of water reconnaissance and hydrographic studies. The Marine Corps in World War II learned the importance of such studies with blood during the Tarawa Campaign.

The Problem

In 1943 the United States was going on the offensive in the Pacific. One of the objectives was the Marshall Islands, which would serve as air bases to further the advance toward Japan. But before they could take the Marshalls, the Americans had to take the Gilberts, which lay in the way and had one operational air base on Betio, part of the atoll called Tarawa.

The commander of the Japanese forces defending Tarawa, Admiral Shibasaki, was so confident of his defenses that he proclaimed that *"a million men cannot take Tarawa in a hundred years."* On an island only a mile long and a few hundred yards wide, he had twenty-six hundred elite Imperial Marines, fourteen coastal defense guns, forty dug-in artillery pieces, and over one hundred well-emplaced machine guns with interlocking fields of fire. The defenders had a four feet high coconut log sea wall covering all approaches to shore.

On the opposite side, the American naval commander (note it was the Navy commander, not the Marine commander) felt equally confident about taking Tarawa: *"We will destroy it,"* he said. *"We will obliterate it."*

This brings to mind one of my team sergeant's Standing Operating Procedures: *"Nothing is impossible to the man who doesn't have to do it."*

The American admiral had reason to be confident: the task force approaching Tarawa consisted of seventeen aircraft carriers, twelve battleships, and numerous supporting ships along with the 2d Marine Division and part of the Army's 37th Division, all told about 35,000 fighting men.

The Admiral had a clear understanding of his What (goal—take the island) and his Why (intent—to control the air base) but he had not studied his Where: Tarawa.

The Solution

At 0215 on 20 November, 1943, the Marines offshore went to General Quarters. They received Last Rites (someone had great, yet depressing foresight) and boarded their landing craft. At 0505 the naval bombardment of Tarawa began. The only times the bombardment paused was to allow dive bombers to get in their licks. The landing craft roared toward the lagoon under the cover of massive fire.

Then things went wrong:

Five hundred yards from shore—five football fields away —the landing craft hit a submerged reef that they could not get over.

At the same time that this unexpected obstacle interfered with the naval commander's plan, the island's Japanese defenders let loose with their entire arsenal of weapons.

The marines, being marines, jumped over the side of

their stranded craft and began to wade ashore. Few in the first wave made it.

Envision what that was like: No planned alternatives. No cover. No concealment. Advancing with heavy loads through water that in some places was over their heads. For over five hundred yards. A running back who gains a hundred yards in a football game is considered to have done something tremendous—but no one's shooting at him, and he isn't in water up to his neck and carrying over a hundred pounds worth of gear. These men were the definition of heroes.

The naval bombardment had caused few casualties among the Japanese, who had hunkered down in bunkers, and then rushed out to their positions during the brief lull between the end of the shelling and the landing.

It took the Marines four successive waves—with the three follow-on waves still coming despite seeing what had happened to those before them—before they were able to establish a tentative toe-hold on the island: they controlled twenty feet inland up to the coconut wall, and a beachhead one hundred yards wide. Less than the size of a football field.

The cost in blood for the poor understanding of the environment surrounding Tarawa was high. Out of five thousand men in the first four waves, over fifteen hundred were dead or wounded.

But the Marines kept coming and by sheer weight of numbers, and outstanding courage, they began to expand the beachhead. In the seventy-six hours it took to conquer the tiny atoll of Tarawa over one thousand Americans died and twenty-three hundred were wounded.

The Lesson

Tarawa was costly in blood, but in the long run it saved lives as the Navy and Marines realized they had to change what they were doing. The Higgins Boats that had been used as landing craft were removed from that task and Amtracs, capable of crawling over reefs such as the one at Tarawa, replaced them.

More importantly, The UDT—Underwater Demolition Teams—the forerunners of the Navy SEALs, were formed to discover natural and man-made obstacles before landings took place. They were formed to conduct Area Studies.

Special Forces Area Study

In Special Forces the first thing we did in mission planning after being given our WHAT (goal) and our WHY (intent) was to conduct a detailed area study. An Area Study is a thorough examination of a the environment. What we call the Area of Operations (AO). We wanted to see what elements in the environment would affect us, and, as importantly, what effect we would have on it.

Ultimately, an area study is the same thing as research.

In Isolation (locked up in a secure compound 24/7 to do mission planning) we'd bring in area experts (CIA agents, State Department personnel, people who'd traveled there, locals, academics, etc) to tell us about the AO. It pays to listen to people who are currently at or have been where you want your path to take you.

The purpose of a Special Forces Area Study is to outline details about the area being studied.

For Special Forces Area Study the following are critical factors:

-Civil populace.

-Military and paramilitary forces.

-Economic factors.

-Political characteristic.

-Resistance forces.

-Geography, hydrography and climate.

-Potential targets.

-Culture, norms, taboos.

In *The Green Beret Preparation and Survival Guide*, the area study is the first step *before* preparation because it is more effective to prepare for most likely threats and scenarios rather than one size fits all.

In the next exercise, you'll do a rudimentary Area Study of your environment. You can do separate ones for your home life, your work environment, your social environment, etc. But in the end, you pull them all together into one complete study of your total environment.

While the Special Operations Forces Area Study is specific to conducting military operations, you can see how you can use this template in your own life. Everything you need for your own path to success has been done by someone else. Yes, you do have to make it specific to your life, but why not use as much of what others have already learned to your advantage? Just as it's important in Special Forces training to study history, you need to study the history that is applicable to your life.

Study those who have succeeded and failed. For example, if you want to be a successful scientist you have to study other scientists, both current and past. How did they achieve what they did? What failures did they encounter on the way, and how did they deal with them?

Overnight successes are few and far between. Among many aspiring writers, I often find an attitude that glittering success can be theirs with just one book. One masterpiece. Yes, that happens once in a while—but it is rare. Most very successful writers spend many years and many books working their way up. They learn the craft and then become artists

Study and research can help shorten the learning curve of your path, and help you avoid the pitfalls that inexperience inevitably brings. This is the reason I am very big on SOPs (Standing Operating Procedures covered in Tool 8).

Consult subject matter experts to get their knowledge and expertise. Study how other people have achieved either exactly what you want to achieve, or goals similar to yours. Your personal area study may actually show you that you can't achieve your successful goal in your environment and thus you have to change your environment.

Jack Canfield, the co-creator of the Chicken Soup books, advises people who want to succeed to get away from toxic people. Sometimes you also need to get away from toxic places.

Your area study of your personal and work environment will identify potential sources of conflict and positive support. Your personal area study helps you define the environment in which you live, the environment's effect on you, and your effect on it.

Take the Challenge: Exercise 6

Take a piece of paper. Fold it in thirds. In the left column
write down the What you listed in column three of
Exercise 4.

Label the middle column *My WHERE As It Is Now.*

Label the right column *My WHERE As It Should Be.*

List in the middle column those people and things that
currently are part of your WHERE and how they effect it.

List in the right column how you would like your
WHERE to be in order to be a positive environment.

Note where there is a large gap between the columns.
The difference between your *As Is* and *Should Be* shows
where you need to change your environment. It shows you
the gap in your life between where you are now and where
you would like to be. The changes that this book will help
you make.

<u>Take the Challenge: Exercise 7</u>
Using the four-column sheet from Exercise 4, fill out the
third column. Next to each WHAT and WHY, list the
WHERE in the third column.

Hopefully, you can see how The Green Beret Guide
exercises will help you break your life and goals into
manageable pieces.

WHERE: The Artist's Imagination
As a writer, part of my area study is the *research* I do for a
book: studying the setting for the book, the characters, the
point of view I'm going to write in, the narrative structure,
etc.

After my students nail down their *What* and *Why*, one
thing I recommend they complete is what I call a Book
Dissection. I have them read a book similar to what they
want to write and analyze it. Not so they can plagiarize the
work—but they need to see how someone else successfully
wrote a book like what they're trying to write.

It's always wise to learn from the masters.

After John Grisham's first novel, *Time to Kill*, failed, he didn't blame his agent, his publisher, bookstores or the reading public. He also didn't quit. He took responsibility. He read a number of bestselling thrillers, analyzed them, and then wrote *The Firm*, which was his breakout book.

I don't restrict the WHERE to the book. I also tell them to do an Area Study of the business environment in which the plan to work. Studying agents, editors, the publishing business, trends, readers, in sum, the entertainment business.

AREA ONE CONCLUSION: WINS
THE GREEN BERET GUIDE

L et's pull together What, Why and Where.
Let me give you two examples, one at a very high level that didn't have positive alignment among the three tools and one at the Special Forces level that did.

NEGATIVE ALIGNMENT EXAMPLE, 1941, Japan versus the United States:

WHAT: The Japanese fleet will destroy the American fleet and change the balance of power in the Pacific.

WHY: The stated Why to this What for Admiral Yamamoto, who commanded the Japanese fleet, was to negate American sea power in the Pacific so the Japanese could conduct other operations. This why was attainable. However, there were those high in the Japanese government who believed the real reason Why they were doing the What of destroying the fleet was to force the United States to sue for peace and retreat from the Pacific theater. This is where alignment started to unravel. Yamamoto, who had traveled extensively in the States, thought this intent was not attainable. He feared, rightly, that the attack would "*awaken a sleeping giant.*" Thus, if his analysis of the hidden Why had been heeded, the What would have had to be changed or dropped.

WHERE: Pearl Harbor. Delving deeper, the Japanese did not do an effective Area Study of their Where to support their What and Why. Even though they were using aircraft carriers to conduct the attack, they did not make certain the American aircraft carriers were present in the harbor on the day of the attack. Instead they focused on the battleships. The very success of their own attack would prove that battleships were obsolete. An inherent paradox the planners did not consider. Also, they could have greatly negated even the not-present carriers ability to carry on operations if they had focused on destroying the port infrastructure rather than just the ships, particularly attacking the massive fuel reserves in the area. Remember when we discussed that Why allows you to innovate? Negating the American fleet could have been done in ways other than trying to directly destroy the fleet, if the planners had done more innovation using the Why.

The Japanese had a spectacular apparent success attacking Pearl Harbor, but there was a subordinate goal under the primary one that they failed to achieve: wiping out the American aircraft carriers, which were at sea during the attack. So both Why's weren't achieved: they did not negate American sea power in the Pacific, because the air power associated with it was intact along with the support infrastructure, especially fuel. As Yamamoto feared, the Americas did not sue for peace. They declared war.

A more careful study of Where might have avoided failure on both Why's and changed the What. First, listening to experts on Americans, such as Yamamoto, the Japanese High Command would have realized the Americans would fight instead of surrender. Second, doing an Area Study of the target just before the attack, they would have learned the aircraft carriers were not present and could have come up with an alternate plan to complete that important part of the plan. They also might have targeted the fuel depots and crippled the fleet indirectly for an extensive period of time. They also might have picked specific targets to sink in the shipping channels of the harbor to deny ingress and egress for an extended period of time.

Do you see how important it is to integrate What, Why and Where?

What the Japanese failed to use is a tool that integrates What, Why and Where: the Special Forces CARVER formula. I cover the Cascade Events building up to Pearl Harbor in more detail in *The Green Beret Guide to Seven Great Disaster (II)*.

Let me describe CARVER to you, then show you an example where it was successfully used.

The CARVER Formula

CARVER is a formula we use in Special Forces to assess targets for specific missions. It is the way we integrate What, Why and Where and come up with the best possible solution for success.

When a Special Forces soldiers gets a mission, he is given the What (goal/target) and Why (intent) and a Where (target and area of operations). He is not told *how* the job is to be done.

The CARVER formula is then applied to assess the target in the following terms:

CRITICALITY: How important is the target? What are the critical nodes of the target? For example, to put a port out of commission for a while, a critical node might be the shipping channel. Or the cranes that load and off-load cargo. Or Pearl Harbor's fuel depot.

ACCESSIBILITY: Can the target be gotten to? How? Can the part of the target that is to be destroyed be accessed? There are often many critical nodes, but some are more easily attacked than others.

RECOGNIZABILITY: Can the target be recognized? Can the critical nodes be located?

VULNERABILITY: Will the team have the capability to actually destroy the target? For example, a dam requires a tremendous amount of force to breach, normally more than a team could carry in. But to overcome this limitation, a team could use a laser designator to guide bombs or cruise missiles to a target. Never accept limitations at first—there are usually ways to overcome them.

EFFECT: What effect outside of the target itself, will the damage have? For example, a team might have the mission to destroy a bridge that the enemy uses to carry supplies over. But will destroying that bridge have too large a negative effect on the population?

RECUPERABILITY: How long will it take to fix the damage done to the target?

CARVER is a way intent can be assessed, tunnel-vision can be avoided, and a *What* could be achieved satisfying the *Why* under the constraints and opportunities of *Where*.

Positive Alignment Example—the A-Team

My team was assigned a mission to destroy a strategic oil

pipeline. We were given the parameters of making the pipeline non-operational for a minimum of seven days.

What: We will destroy the pipeline.

Why: To deny the enemy oil from it for seven days.

Where: We were given a specified length of the pipeline from which to pick the point we wanted to attack in order to achieve our What and Why.

The Problem

We learned that destroying a normal section of the pipe would achieve the What (destroy the pipeline) but not achieve that Why: the repair estimate for a damaged section was forty-eight hours. Just walking up to the pipe and blowing it was out.

The Solution

The demolitions men began searching for *critical nodes* doing an Area Study (Where). The thing about critical nodes in targets though, is that the people who own the target also usually recognize these spots and put extra security on them. We knew destroying a pump station would achieve the Why, but the pump stations were well-guarded. The odds of successfully destroying one with the assets we had on the team were limited.

We looked at the pipeline terminus to see if we could destroy the means by which the oil was transferred out of the pipeline and onto further conveyances. However, we were denied attacking the port because the effect would have been greater than simply taking out the pipeline.

Even though an attack blocking the channel to oil tankers would have achieved the What and Why, we couldn't do it. It would have achieved other undesirable effects, including severe environmental damage.

We kept looking, going along the hundreds of miles of pipeline imagery. Then we found it. The pipeline crossed rivers in two places. Over one of those rivers the pipeline was held up by a suspension bridge consisting of two towers and cables. We consulted with experts (Area Study research) and learned that if we blew the cables, the weight of the oil in the length of pipe suspended over the river would be too much to sustain and that section would rip free.

The repair timeline on the pipe over the river was different than that for the pipe on the ground, as a barge with a crane would have to be brought up river. Estimates ranged from one week to two.

Security at the crossing was a barbed wire fence and video surveillance, both of which we could overcome. Apparently the enemy did not realize the significance of this site and had no security force on it.

The Result

We did have to consider the ecological effect of the oil that would be let loose into the river, but the nearest pump station was only a few miles away and as soon pressure was lost on the pipe, the pump station would shut down.

We had our critical node that satisfied CARVER. We could achieve the assigned goal.

CARVER and Your Goals

Sometimes CARVER led my Special Forces team to change a mission goal. When you start researching your environment (in your area study) and examining your intent, don't be disturbed if you end up adjusting your goals as well.

CARVER is not a step-by-step process, but rather an overview and interactive. The questions in CARVER can be answered in any order. You'll develop all the answers you need as you work through nine tools within your Circle of Success.

To expand your personal area study, ask yourself these CARVER questions:

CRITICALITY:

- How important is my goal?
- What are the critical parts (nodes) of my goal?
- What is the key to achieving this goal?
- How many other people can do what I want to achieve?

ACCESSIBILITY:

- Can the goal be achieved?
- Can it be achieved with my available resources?
- How can I get to the goal from where I am now?
- If this access point is a *critical node*, can I actually reach it?

RECOGNIZABILITY:

- Can I clearly see my goal and state it?
- Do I clearly know the WHY I want to achieve this goal?
- How can I get side-tracked in achieving my goal?

- Will the process of achieving my goal overwhelm the end result?

VULNERABILITY:

- Am I capable of achieving my goal?
- If I don't have the capability, what help is needed?
- Do I have the resources to achieve my goal?
- If I don't have the resources, what help is needed?

EFFECT:

- What effect will achieving my goal have on me?
- What effect will achieving my goal have on those around me?
- What effect will achieving my goal have on my environment?

RECUPERABILITY:

- Will my effort achieve the desired results?
- What are the possible undesired results?
- Can I sustain my effort, or will I revert to old habits?

<u>Take the Challenge: Exercise 8</u>
Using the four-column sheet from Exercise 4, fill out the third column. Next to each WHAT and WHY, list the WHERE in the third column.
Using your four column sheet from Exercise 4, pick one of the What's. Using the Why and Where you've already added, apply the CARVER formula to the goal to see if you can achieve it. If you can, then you can check column four—Done.
This doesn't mean the What is actually done; it means your planning for it is done. You can apply this formula to all your Whats.

Now that you have an idea of *what* your goals are, *why* you want to achieve your goals, and how to refine your *what* and *why* based on *where* you will be operating, it's time to move to Area Two: WHO.

AREA TWO: WHO

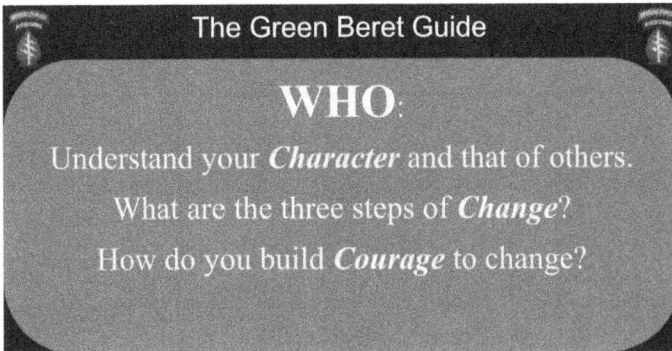

We'll start with CHARACTER so you understand yourself and others. Then learn what true CHANGE is and how to accomplish it. And finally learn how you can utilize COURAGE to conquer fear and be the person you want to be.

Character is the essence of a person. Your character is made up of both your strengths and your weaknesses. It's important to understand yourself, especially your blind spot, before taking action to achieve your goals. Your blind spot is wrapped around your deepest fears. A successful individual doesn't ignore fear, but rather faces it, plans for it, and factors it into their life with courage.

Most of What You Do Is Habit

The tools in the Green Beret Guide help you consciously change your habits, and through the Circle of Success, your life. You have to train yourself to question your repeated behaviors.

I'm not talking radical, burning bush type change that will occur instantaneously. This book teaches you incremental, day-by-day change. Small changes, added together, day-after-day, that lead to new habits and a new life. Your focus will not only be on the end result, but on the continuous process. When you finish Tool Nine, you won't be done, but you will be changed.

I focus a great deal on fear for someone who is teaching about success, because changing habits is not for the faint of heart. Most of us like comfort and security.

A little change brings discomfort. A lot of change brings fear. There is a very thin line between discomfort and fear. The more you are willing to face and conquer your fears, the further out you push that line and the more change you'll bring about as you venture further into your Courage Zone, which increases your Comfort Zone. In fact, as you'll learn, there are benefits to fear.

TOOL FOUR: UNDERSTAND YOUR CHARACTER AND THAT OF OTHERS

Y ou need to understand your own character as it is now, before you set off to change. Being aware of your flaws and blind spots is key. These can trip you up when you start pursuing your life goals.

Not understanding your complete character, can lead to goals and a path generated by fear—a recipe for failure, not success.

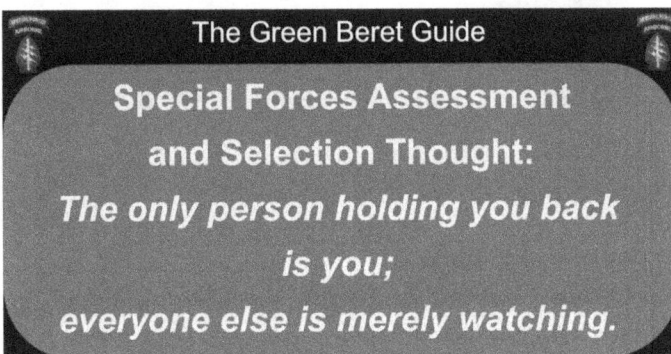

The Green Beret Guide

Special Forces Assessment and Selection Thought:
The only person holding you back is you;
everyone else is merely watching.

Blood Lesson: Never Give Up

Let's look at *Character* profiles for two legendary Special Forces officers.

The Problem

Nick Rowe: 1960, graduated from West Point; 1963, went to Vietnam, Special Forces, at a time when most Americans couldn't tell you where Vietnam was. October 29, 1963, he was on patrol with Captain 'Rocky' Versace and Sergeant Daniel Pitzer, advising a Civilian Irregular Defense Group company, searching for a small enemy unit reportedly in the area.

Captain Versace: on his second tour in Vietnam, after volunteering to stay to help the people he loved; accepted to the seminary upon his return. Only two weeks away from coming back to the States, he volunteered for the October 29th patrol.

At ten in the morning, the patrol's pursuit of the enemy triggered an ambush. After fighting until late afternoon, the unit was over-run and the two officers were captured. The Vietcong's focus was to break American captive's will—so they could extract tactical information.

The Solutions

Captain 'Rocky' Versace:
Captain Humbert R. Versace distinguished himself by extraordinary heroism during the period of 29 October 1963 to 26 September 1965, while serving as S-2 Advisor, Military Assistance Advisory Group, Detachment 52, Ca Mau, Republic of Vietnam. While accompanying a Civilian Irregular Defense Group patrol

engaged in combat operations in Thoi Binh District, An Xuyen Province, Captain Versace and the patrol came under sudden and intense mortar, automatic weapons, and small arms fire from elements of a heavily armed enemy battalion.

As the battle raged, Captain Versace, although severely wounded in the knee and back by hostile fire, fought valiantly and continued to engage enemy targets. Weakened by his wounds and fatigued by the fierce firefight, Captain Versace stubbornly resisted capture by the over-powering Viet Cong force with the last full measure of his strength and ammunition. Taken prisoner by the Viet Cong, he exemplified the tenets of the Code of Conduct from the time he entered into Prisoner of War status. Captain Versace assumed command of his fellow American soldiers, scorned the enemy's exhaustive interrogation and indoctrination efforts, and made three unsuccessful attempts to escape, despite his weakened condition which was brought about by his wounds and the extreme privation and hardships he was forced to endure.

During his captivity, Captain Versace was segregated in an isolated prisoner of war cage, manacled in irons for prolonged periods of time, and placed on extremely reduced ration. The enemy was unable to break his indomitable will, his faith in God, and his trust in the United States of America. Captain Versace, an American fighting man who epitomized the principles of his country and the Code of Conduct, was executed by the Viet Cong on 26 September 1965. Captain Versace's gallant actions in close contact with an enemy force and unyielding courage and bravery while a prisoner of war are in the highest traditions of the military service and reflect the utmost credit upon himself and the United States Army.

Captain Versace exemplified the true spirit of the Special Forces soldier, both in combat, and in captivity. Despite the two radically different situations, he remained consistent and true to his character. When he was isolated from the other prisoners they knew he was still there because he would sing God Bless America at the top of his lungs. In his first attempt to escape, because of wounds to his legs, he crawled.

Nick Rowe

Nick Rowe spent sixty-two months in captivity. Every day he could expect to face the same fate as his friend. He suffered from dysentery, beri-beri, fungal diseases, malnutrition, and torture. He lived in a wooden cage three feet by four by six.

When interrogated, Rowe deceived the Vietcong about his background. He told them he was a draftee and an engineer and his job was to build schools. He said he had gone to a small liberal college. To test him, the Vietcong gave him engineering problems to solve. Because West Point had numerous mandatory engineering courses, Rowe passed these tests. Rowe's cover story was eventually blown through no fault of his own.

An American anti-war activist group came to North Vietnam. They asked to speak to POWs to see if they were being treated fairly. On the top of their list was Rowe's name, along with his real background and assignment. Note, that this group had failed to do an effective area study of where they were going and the effect their actions went beyond the immediate result they desired--with almost tragic results.

Rowe was taken out into a swamp and staked down naked for two days. He still refused talk, even though the information he knew was now dated and useless. He later escaped with another wounded POW. Chased and about to be caught, the other POW urged Rowe to go on. He did so, but stopped when he heard the Vietcong calling out that they would execute the man if he did not come back, so he came back.

Would you have done the same?

In December 1968, over five years after he'd been captured, Rowe was taken out to be executed. The Vietcong had had enough, and they knew any information he had was long past worthless.

As they took him to the place of his death, several American helicopters flew overhead. Rowe took advantage of the diversion, striking down his guards and running into a clearing. Despite being malnourished and dressed in black pajamas, he was recognized as a westerner. A helicopter swooped down and picked him up.

In 1971 he published his story, *Five Years To Freedom,* and retired from active duty to write full-time. But in 1981, his country reached out to him. Realizing he had a unique expertise, he was brought to the JFK Special Warfare Center & School at Fort Bragg to design a training course called SERE: Survival, Evasion, Resistance and Escape. The course is still in existence today and has helped thousands of American soldiers.

The Lesson

Versace and Rowe are classic examples of men who exerted strong personal *Character* under adverse conditions. Yes, these were extreme examples, but in your life you will face extreme tests in various ways to your Character. Both Versace and Rowe became men who exhibited such Courage not only because of innate abilities, but also because of the training they received as Green Berets.

No matter what pressure was brought on them, what their level of fear was, they stayed true to what they believed in. Equally important: they remained true to their comrades.

What is Character?

Character is the combination of qualities or features that distinguishes one person from another. Character is the key to looking at the world around you differently than others and understanding yourself.

Too many people are locked into a limited worldview, because their own character keeps them from seeing the true nature of the world around them. Your view of others and the world around you is colored by your point of view. If you understand your point of view, you'll have a more realistic view of yourself and others.

Take the Challenge: Exercise 9
Define Yourself in one sentence.

Which of the following areas did you use in your definition?

• Work

- Position
- Family
- Background
- Schooling
- Education level
- Marital status
- Sexual orientation
- Age
- Race

Do you define others by the same, or different, terms? You are now getting an idea of your point of view. Remember, everyone doesn't share your point of view. Understanding your point of view shapes the way you view of others and makes your reality different than their reality.

Study Your Actions To Understand Your Character.

In Special Forces, we learned that a person tends to show his true nature by their actions/reactions during a crisis. You learn a lot about people by observing what choices they make under pressure.

Actions are a WHAT. As we learned in Area One, you should also try to figure out the corresponding WHY for each WHAT. The same WHAT done for two different WHYs (intent), makes the actions very different.

Not only must you observe an action and the intent, you must have an understanding of the environment the action is taken in (WHERE) to help you interpret motivation (WHY).

In schools such as Special Forces Assessment & Selection, Ranger School, Dive School, Jumpmaster School, etc. this basic tenet of acting under constant stress and crisis is drilled into students while they are performing under extreme pressure. Incoming plebes' first summer at West Point is called 'Beast Barracks;' which gives you an idea of the environment they face.

The harshness of this kind of training is often explained by saying the instructors must first 'break a person down,' before they can rebuild them. I believe this method strips away any façade a person has and drills down to his true nature.

Understand Your True Nature

Those whose true nature cannot handle a specific situation will either quit or fail. People who do not succeed in Beast Barracks, Ranger School, SEAL training, Special Forces and SAS Assessment & Selection, etc. are not bad people or failures. They just do not belong in the environments those training programs are designed to prepare them for. In the same way, you have to understand your true nature, so you can choose a path of change you are capable of completing. Keep in mind that this harsh phase of breaking someone down is a form of making the person surrender. The more the person fights the change, the harsher the resulting process. To change, you have to surrender to the fact that who you are now and what you're doing isn't working. And that the more you fight yourself, the more that fight will be projected into your world with harsh, negative effects.

Take the Challenge: Exercise 10

On the same sheet as Exercise 9, describe a moment when you were under extreme stress and pressure and had to make a decision. List the cause of the stress and pressure.

Take the Challenge: Exercise 11

On the same sheet as exercises 9 and 10, describe your reaction to that moment and the decision you made. In retrospect, was it a good decision, or could you have chosen better?

Your Primary Motivator

People who are successful have a readily identifiable primary motivator that allows them to overcome great obstacles and succeed. These people who have a meaning in their life can transcend suffering and find success. They can live well in the face of fear.

Some people might already have their meaning of life. Others may need to find one.

In Special Forces training, the candidates are forced to perform under extreme duress. They not only accept challenges, but conquer them. They're forced to dig deep, to find what really motivates them. The desire just to wear a green beret and call themselves Special Forces doesn't work. Those candidates who want the superficial aspects because of the way others will view them fall to the wayside. In the same way as an author, I've noticed many people want what they think the lifestyle of an author is, but they don't have the wherewithal to *be* an author.

In the beginning of this book, you were asked to write down what motivates you the most in Exercise 2. Look back at your answer. Is it truly your primary motivator?

Successful Character Traits

Special Forces Assessment and Selection is based on successful character traits. Studying some of these will help you understand your True Nature.

Open Mindedness

How willing are you to change? Are you willing to learn from any source that helps you improve yourself? If you are not where you want to be, then you must change something, rather than waiting for the world to come to you.

Because guess what?

It isn't.

So how do you use being open-minded to change? You need a . . .

Willingness to Surrender When Wrong

To change, you have to be willing to say the three hardest words for many people: "*I am wrong.*" Followed by, "*Maybe I'm not doing this the best possible way. Maybe I can learn to do this better.*" You must be willing to change based on the feedback you receive from the exercises in this book.

A Stanford psychologist, Carol Dweck, found something interesting when studying talented people and how they performed. She discovered that those people who believe they were born with all the talent and intelligence they need approach the world with a *fixed* mind-set. They rarely change. Why should they?

Those who believe that they weren't born with everything they need and can expand their abilities and become better, approach the world with a *growth* mind-set. Guess which of the two are more successful? The latter reach their creative potential, while the former rarely live up to their potential. In Special Forces, volunteering for the training and successfully completing it indicates a willingness to grow. I found the same to be true of writers: I often saw extremely talented writers fail, while those with lesser talent but greater open-mindedness and perseverance succeed.

Change is also difficult because it requires not just change in your action but also . . .

Emotional Change

Once you've accepted the need for change and surrendered your current position and mental outlook, you've intellectually accepted the change. You then change your actions, which we will discuss in more detail further in this book. As you change it effects you emotionally over time.

Emotional change can take years but you have to stick with it.

Change requires five emotional stages.

1. DENIAL: there is no problem or need to change.

2. ANGER: how dare someone, including me, say I'm not doing it right.

3. BARGAINING: maybe if I can change some small things it will make a big difference.

4. DEPRESSION: There's too much to change. I'm overwhelmed.

5. ACCEPTANCE: I will do it. Which does lead to real change.

Note that these are Elizabeth Kubler-Ross's stages of death and dying! To change you have to 'kill' off your old self.

Take the Challenge: Exercise 12
Describe the last time you were told you were doing something wrong and how you responded to it.

**Describe your reaction in terms of the five parts of the Kubler-Ross scale.
Did you make it to acceptance and change?
If not, where did you stop and why?**

If you didn't, don't worry. This book will help you get there and change. Remember, that's Tool 5, coming next.

Part of what can motivate you to try change and also stick with it are two apparently paradoxical emotions . . .

Desire & Contentment

Desire is the stick that drives the successful to achieve more. The carrot. What do you desire? What do you want?

Note I say want, not need. There is a big difference between a need and a want. A need is something that you don't have control over desiring. A want is something you can control.

A successful individual must climb above his needs and focus on his wants.

Contentment is the reward for achieving your desires. You can't constantly be in a state of desire all the time. Every once in a while you must get to that point of achievement, or frustration will rule. For a person to enjoy life, there must be a degree of contentment in the here and now. What is the point of being successful if you can't enjoy it? Every once in a while you need to focus on what has been achieved.

A successful person needs to balance desire and contentment.

Take the Challenge: Exercise 13
Take a piece of paper. Draw a line down the middle. Label
the left side TO DO. Label the right side DONE.
List down the left side everything you have to do
tomorrow.
Then, when you do one of your TO DO's, cross it off *and*
write what you've done on the right side. Thus you can
literally see your balance between desire and
contentment on one page for one day.

Use this technique on a daily basis to give yourself positive feedback. Crossing something off a list isn't quite as
satisfying emotionally as listing something achieved.

As part of desire and contentment, you must also be able
to 'close doors'. We waste time pursuing too many options.
One of the purposes of the first Area of this book was to
help you lock down your WHAT, your goals. Discarding
goals that aren't what you really want can help you focus on
those you do.

The French philosopher Jean Buridan tells this parable
known as Buridan's Ass: a hungry donkey enters a barnyard.
There are equal sized bales of hay to either side. The
donkey remains frozen, unable to chose one, afraid that by

doing so, it will not get the other. Eventually the donkey starves to death.

Ever felt like that donkey?

Closing doors can give you great focus. When we have too many options, we don't focus on the ones we should.

<u>Take the Challenge: Exercise 14</u>
Look at your TO DO/DONE list from Exercise 13. Are there some TO DO's that aren't really needed? That you've actually had on your TO DO list a long time and never gotten around to? Maybe you shouldn't do them at all. Close some doors. Get rid of options that distract from your main goals.

Patience and Self-Discipline

Too many people rely on the outside world to enforce patience and supply discipline. A successful person internalizes both traits. The Special Forces Qualification Course takes roughly sa year. Interestingly, the average time many authors spend on a novel is a year. Neither are a recipe for instant gratification. Taking a year to achieve a goal is something that requires a great deal of patience and discipline.

When I taught martial arts, the majority of the new students quit shortly after the first month. Students came in and wanted to become Bruce Lee rolled into Chuck Norris, all within a couple of weeks. When they realized it would take years of boring, repetitive, very hard work, the majority gave up. It doesn't take any special skill up front to become a black belt—just a lot of time and effort to develop special skills. The same is true of pretty much anything you want to achieve.

If you are patient enough to do the long-term work, you will pull ahead of the pack and become successful. Which means you must have a long-term perspective of your major goals.

To keep focus on long-term work, you must accept that the pay-off usually comes later, rather than sooner. Delayed gratification is one of the keys to self-discipline.

One way to make a long-term goal achievable and not overwhelming, is to break it down into subordinate goals that are closer and more easily achievable. For example, in the Special Forces Qualification Course there are numerous phases. As a candidate passes each phase they feel a sense of accomplishment, leading to passing the entire course. Also, if a candidate has a problem in a particular phase, there is always the option to have them redo just that phase, rather than the entire course. As a writer, I can break a book down to number of pages to write per day or a number of chapters per month. I can write a scene, just to get the bones of it down, and then come back to it, improving the writing.

An Active Imagination

Make your creative plans based on acting within your character--much like chess strategy is dependent on a piece being capable of a specific type of move—and then, once you've mastered that, press the limits of your character to expand your capabilities—venturing into your Courage Zone. You'll get an idea of your character template shortly and how to expand what I call your Comfort Zone (Tool 5— next) so that you are capable of more and more 'moves'.

Set your imagination free to plot numerous paths. From these, based on all the variables facing you, you can choose the one that stands out above the others—the successful or critical path.

As in chess, a successful person in life must be able to see a problem in its entirety, and then be able to break a solution down into manageable steps. You must be able to see beyond the current move, to each move's implications.

Don't get tunnel vision. For example, a visiting professor from the Colorado School of Mines teaching at West Point once presented his students with a problem to test their imaginations:

A two-foot metal pipe is welded vertically to a steel plate. It is just barely wide enough to slide a ping-pong ball into. The class's job is to get the ball out of the pipe without damaging the ball. The only tools given the students are a pair of pliers, a coat hanger, a magnet, and a comb.

The professor let the class war-game this problem for a while, then listened to various proposals, none of which worked. His solution used none of the tools listed—he'd given them as distracters. To get the ball out, simply urinate into the pipe until the ball floated out. But because we'd been given those tools, every solution focused on using those items rather than the problem.

The Ability To Set Goals

In *Area One: Wins,* you learned the importance of specifying your goals, understanding why you want to achieve them, and studying the situation in which you want to become successful.

One thing you can do without is procrastination. It comes from two Latin words:

Pro: For. Cras: Tomorrow.

Not only must you set your goals (WHAT), you must also set deadlines for your goals. People with firm deadlines written down get better results than those without.

<u>Take the Challenge: Exercise 15</u>
Remember the four column What, Why, Where, Done list
you began in Exercise 4? For every What that has not been
Done, pencil in a deadline for when it should be done.
The clock is now ticking.

Emotion and Intellect

As an author I work in the entertainment business, which is an oxymoron. Entertainment runs on emotion, while business runs on logic (supposedly). But no matter what business you're in, emotion plays a significant factor that can't be quantified.

Why is a certain book a bestseller and another not? Why does one movie break box office records and another doesn't? If the answers to these questions could be put into a formula, then everyone would be following the formula and every book would be a bestseller. Every movie would be a blockbuster.

Why do we do things that ultimately hurt ourselves? In lucid moments we know they make no sense. But then we go out and do whatever it is anyway. In these situations, emotion is overwhelming your logic. Many individuals and organizations don't value the power of emotion.

It is important to realize there are two sets of norms in your life: Social Norms and Market Norms. Your personal relationships belong in the realm of social norms. Social norms are based on emotion. Your business relationships are in the realm of market norms. Market norms are based on money.

When a market norm collides with a social norm, the social norm is the loser and is easily subsumed and very hard to recover. For example, if you offered your spouse money after they picked you up at the airport, you would be bringing a market norm into the social realm and your spouse would most likely be offended. It would not be something easily forgotten.

Conversely, social norms are more powerful than market norms in terms of motivation. This comes into play in The Green Beret Guide, because, interestingly enough, Special Forces operates more on Social Norms than Market Norms. Jobs where one is asked to put his or her life on the line can't function well under Markets Norms—how much can you

pay someone for their life? Thus police, firefighters and
military tend to operate under Social Norms where pride in
profession, team-work and care for comrades, and a sense of
duty are more important than money.

A curious case exists regarding professional athletes
where coaches face the difficult job of trying to merge both
social norms (for motivation and team-building) with
market norms (because it is a business). There is a trend
nowadays for more businesses to try to bring Social Norms
into the work place. While this can be very effective, it can
also be very dangerous, if there is not consistency in the
application of the Social Norms in the work environment.

In your life, recognize that the way you interact with
other people emotionally—social norms—is much more
important than any market norms interaction.

Anger and Guilt

Two emotional blind spots for many people are anger and
guilt. These emotions are often indicators of a weakness you
need to deal with. And until you do, that weakness can keep
you from exploring your full potential, and can derail you
from achieving your goals.

Whenever you experience anger or guilt, focus on what
is going on. Figure out when the emotion is appropriate,
and understand when it isn't.

Anger and guilt are often brought about by things that
normally shouldn't trigger it: frequently, these emotions are
responses that became a habit in childhood. While both are
necessary at times, many people are so consumed by these
negative emotions, they becomes a shackle around their
lives.

When a person gets angry about something someone

else is doing, it is often a sign of a flaw in the angry person's character. When a person feels guilty about something happening in their life, it is often an inappropriate response to reality. We use these two in Special Forces training to build a person's character:

Flash Points

During prisoner of war (SERE-survival, evasion, resistance and escape) training (developed by Colonel Rowe) run by Special Forces, one thing the instructors do to participants is find their flash points—what makes a prisoner react angrily or with guilt.

If captors can find a prisoner's flash point and exploit it, they can delve deeper and find the prisoner's greatest fears. This allows the captors to break the prisoner much more quickly. Left unchallenged, your mind can become it's own kind of prison, where your flash points and greatest fears will work against you with increasing frequency.

The key to the training is that once the candidate goes through this experience and is aware of his or her flash point, they can strengthen themselves in those areas and are less likely to react to a flash point in the future and in a real SERE situation.

Anger and guilt spring out of fear, usually on a subconscious level. You'll learn later that working through your mind's defense barriers is the second step of emotional change. As you become more conscious of your blind spots and flaws, you gain more control over them.

<u>Take the Challenge: Exercise 16</u>
Describe the last time you felt anger or guilt? (If you can't remember, then try to focus on the *next* time you feel either of those emotions). Write the event down. What specifically provoked the emotion? Why did this situation touch your flash point? Simply understanding this dynamic will make you stronger the next time your flash point is touched.

Character Templates

Successful individuals adopt a psychological structure for character types—so they can better understand their own character and others'. Fortunately, structures already exist and have been thoroughly developed by behavior and motivation experts. I recommend studying various templates and recommend two here:

Profiling

Character type profiling is regularly used by Special Forces and law enforcement, a fact that has been repeatedly fictionalized in pop culture books, movies and television. A profiler examines the results of an action and works backwards, trying to come up with the character type that would perform such an act.

When Special Forces was founded, a list of character traits for the type of person needed to operate in this elite unit was drawn up based on experiences in guerilla warfare and covert operations in World War II. Then they looked for those types of people.

A key to profiling is that it shows that people have character traits that dictate their actions. This is understandable because most of what we do is habit. Also, the brain doesn't start from scratch in every situation—we have imprinted stereotypes that shape our actions. We consciously control very little of our day to day life and decision-making.

The founders of the Behavioral Science branch of the FBI began their study of profiling by going to prisons and interviewing every living serial killer, to see what type of person was capable of doing such horrible acts. Patterns were identified in the killers' backgrounds, their thought processes, the way they conducted their crimes, etc. In the same manner, you can study patterns in your and others' daily lives. One of those founders has an interesting book about this, titled *Mindhunter*.

You can determine which of your life patterns are positive, and which are negative, then work on getting rid of the negative ones, and replace them with positive ones.

By profiling yourself, you can make more conscious choices, rather than react emotionally and out of blind habit.

<u>Take the Challenge: Exercise 17</u>
For the next 24 hours, write down everything you do.
Simply list every action, and how long it took, without
comment. Let the list sit for several days. Then look at the
list with an open mind. Describe what kind of person
would do these things?
Then answer these questions: "Is this the kind of person I
want to be? Are these the things I really want to be
spending my time doing?"

The Myers-Briggs

Many of you have probably taken a Myers-Briggs assessment. It was developed in the dark days of World War II
when it was necessary to assess a large numbers of people
quickly in order to position them in the best jobs for their
personality.

It is not a test, but an indicator of Character type. There
are four areas to it, with two possible orientations, which
totals sixteen Character types. To give you a brief idea where
you stand do the following four exercises. While this does
not replace the standard test (which can be found on-line or
in a book *Please Understand Me: Temperament, Character,*

Intelligence) the following exercise can put you in the ball-park for our purposes:

Take the Challenge: Exercise 18
Pick A or B for each of the four areas that best describe you:

Area 1

Block A	Block B
Act first, think later?	Think first, then act?
Feel deprived if cut off from world?	Need private time to get energized?
Motivated by outside world?	Internally motivated?
Get energized by groups?	Groups drin your energy?

Area 2

Block A	Block B
Mentally live in the now?	Mentally live in the future?
Use common sense for practical solutions?	Use imagination for innovative solutions?
Memory focuses on details and facts?	Memory focuses on patterns and context?
Don't like guessing?	Like guessing?

Area 3

Block A	Block B
Search for facts to make a decision?	Go with feelings on making a decision?
Notice work to be accomplished?	Focus on people's needs?
Tend to provide an objective analysis?	Seek consensus and popular opinion?
Believe conflict is all right?	Dislike conflict and avoid it at all costs?

Area 4

Block A	Block B
Plan detail before taking action?	Are comfortable taking action without a plan?
Complete tasks in order?	Like to multi-task?
Stay ahead of deadlines?	Work best close to deadlines?
Set goals, deadlines and routines?	Like to be flexible and avoid commitments?

The results:
1A= Extrovert (E)1B= Introvert (I)
2A= Sensing (S)2B= iNtuition (N)
3A= Thinking (T)3B= Feeling (F)
4A= Judging (J)4B= Perceiving (P)
List out you four letters. You are one of sixteen Myers-Briggs Character types:

Myers-Briggs Types

INTP= Architect	ESJF= Seller
ENTP= Inventor	ISFJ= Conservator
INTJ= Scientist	ESFP= Entertainer
ENTJ= Field Marshall	ISFP= Artist
INFP= Questor	ESTJ= Administrator
ENFP= Journalist	ISTJ= Trustee
INFJ= Author	ESTP= Promoter
ENJF= Pedagogue	ISTP= Artisan

The first letter is extroversion vs introversion. This is how you view the world. E's are social while I's are territorial. E's prefer breath and a wide variety while I's prefer depth and one on one. E's tend to be externally motivated while I's tend to be internally motivated. 75% of people are E's, while 25% are I's.

The second letter is iNtuition vs. Sensation. N's tend to be innovative while S's are practical. This area is the greatest source of misunderstanding between people. 25% of people are N's while 75% are S's.

The third letter is Thinking vs. Feeling. T's analyze and decide in a detached manner, while F's analyze and decide in an emotional manner. Basically T's are logical while F's are emotional. It's 50-50 in the population but overall more women are Feeling and more men are Thinking.

The fourth letter is Judging vs. Perceiving. J's like closure while P's like things open-ended. J's like the result while P's like the process. It's also 50-50 in the population.

Looking at your Character type can give you an idea of

yourself. It shows you how you interact with other people. How you take in information. How you make decisions. How you view processes.

It is very important to look at what the exact opposite of your character type is and you'll get an idea of your blind spots and your weaknesses. I learned this as a writer:

CHARACTER: The Artist's Imagination

I began my second career as an author being a plot-driven writer. It took me ten years and a lot of hard work before I saw that I was going about things the wrong way. In the same way that in Special Forces we put people first, a writer has to do the same thing in novels—put the characters first.

People relate more to people, not things.

Think about your favorite novel. What do you remember the most? It is most likely the characters, not the plot. When writing a novel, I want my main character to have 'arc'. This means the character changes. Just like you will change by implementing the tools in this book.

In a novel, if you thrust the main character into the climactic scene as he exists at the beginning of the novel, the character should fail. The journey that character goes through in the story should change him, so that when he faces the antagonist in the climactic scene, the main character will win.

The same change will be required in your life, if you want to succeed in the critical moments you committed yourself to facing when you set your goals. You must step out of your comfort zone and do things that are inherently against your nature so you can conquer fear and succeed.

Another enlightening experience for me was to look at the Myers-Briggs types noting I was an INFJ (author), and noting what the exact opposite type, ESTP, was: promoter. This made me see some of my blind spots and forced me to work to get out of my comfort zone and into my fear zone to promote my books and business. It also required me to ask for assistance in areas I was weak in.

TOOL FIVE: WHAT IS CHANGE
AND HOW DO YOU DO IT?

I f you aren't where you want to be, then you must change. How many people do you know who have really changed? Your answer will ultimately depend on what you think *change* is.

I can tell you what change isn't: change is not simply thinking differently. Thinking doesn't change anything in the world outside of your mind. Here comes my next paradox, though—the first step of change is to think differently.

An official definition of change is to make or become different. There's a big difference between the verbs *make* and *become*. It's the difference between being ordinary and successful:

- *Make* is externally imposed.
- *Become* is internally motivated.

The successful become.

Can people change? If the answer to that is no, then there is no purpose to this book and we all might as well quit now. There's good news, though--history has proven that people CAN change. Change is very difficult and very few people manage to achieve great change in their life and sustain it. These people are the successful.

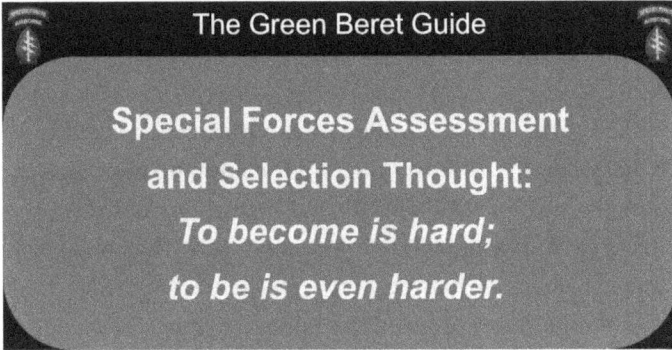

> ### The Green Beret Guide
>
> ## Special Forces Assessment and Selection Thought:
> *To become is hard;*
> *to be is even harder.*

Blood Lesson: From Scholar to Warrior to Scholar to Politician

"But we can hold our spirits and our bodies so pure and high, we may cherish such thoughts and ideals, and dream such dreams of lofty purpose, that we can determine and know what manner of men we will be, whenever and wherever the hour strikes and calls to noble action."

Joshua Chamberlain.

The Problem

The Civil War was fought primarily by volunteers. At the start of the war there were only 1,080 Regular Army officers. There was an urgent need for officers as the army exploded in size. Where did these men come from? How could one change from whatever civilian job a man held, to become a military officer commanding thousands of soldiers in combat? How could one man make the radical change from seminary professor to soldier?

The Solution

Officers were found in many places, but they were mostly political appointees. Some units even elected their own officers. Since most new officers had little or no military background, there were no guidelines to appoint people on merit.

An officer who made one of the greatest changes from civilian life to military life, and commanded the most strategic position at the pivotal battle of Gettysburg—enabling the Union to eventually win the war—was Lawrence Joshua Chamberlain from Maine.

Chamberlain was given the name Lawrence, in honor of Commodore James Lawrence, whose famous saying was "Don't give up the ship!" while battling the British during the War of 1812. Perhaps his parents had great foresight because Chamberlain would take those words to heart later in life, not at sea, but on a small hill in southern Pennsylvania.

As a child working the rough fields of Maine, he learned that strength of character, followed by sustained willpower in action, could bring about change. His father wanted him to go to the Military Academy at West Point, while his mother preferred for him to study for the ministry—a rather wide gulf in possible career paths. Mother prevailed when Chamberlain entered Bowdoin College. Perhaps as a sign of his change in path, he began using Joshua as his first name, dropping the military-heritage first name. As a student, he earned a reputation for sticking to his principles, even when challenged by authority.

After graduating, Chamberlain took a position teaching rhetoric and oratory at Bowdoin. When the Civil War broke out, he had a great desire to enlist. But the Bowdoin College administration felt he was too valuable to be given permission to do this. They granted him a leave of absence to study language abroad in Europe for two years. Chamberlain left the school and promptly enlisted.

He was offered command of the 20th Maine, but declined saying he needed to "start a little slower and learn the business first." He was appointed a Lieutenant Colonel and served under a recent West Point graduate to learn how to be an officer. Chamberlain learned so well, he eventually *earned* command of the 20th Maine, leading to his fateful encounter with destiny.

On 2 July 1863, the 20th Maine was put in position on the far left flank of the Union Army at Gettysburg. Chamberlain was ordered to hold a hill, Little Round Top, at all costs. He did so, until his unit's ammunition was nearly depleted and his men exhausted.

Chamberlain then did something one would least expect in such dire straits: he ordered his men to fix bayonets and attack. So stunning was this move that the equally exhausted Confederate soldiers, who had been attacking all day, broke. Chamberlain had saved the left flank: and the Union Army.

In April, 1864, Chamberlain was so severely wounded in battle, that General Grant gave him a posthumous promotion to Brigadier General. The posthumous was a bit premature, since Chamberlain survived his wound. Chamberlain fought in 20 battles and numerous skirmishes, was cited for bravery four times, had six horses shot from under him, and was wounded six times. He'd come a long way from being the ministry student.

At the end of the war, when General Lee surrendered to General Grant at Appomattox, Grant selected Chamberlain to preside over the formal surrender parade of Confederate

Infantry. As the defeated Confederates marched by to lay down their arms and colors, Chamberlain had his men come to attention and present arms as a sign of respect. The Confederate commander in turn had his men return the gesture: the seeds of reconciliation were sown by these simple, respectful gestures, initiated by a former ministry student and college professor who had evolved into one of the best officers in the Union Army.

After the war, Chamberlain, bored with the academic life and much changed by his wartime experiences, ran for governor of Maine and won by the largest majority in the State's history. He served four consecutive terms.

The Lesson

Thirty year after the end of the Civil War, Chamberlain was awarded the Medal of Honor for his actions on Little Round Top:

Here's the text of his citation: *Daring heroism and great tenacity in holding his position on the Little Round Top against repeated assaults, and carrying the advance position on the Great Round Top.*

Simple and to the point, just like the man.

Because Joshua Chamberlain was willing to learn and change his actions, he achieved great things as a scholar, a soldier and a statesman.

But how exactly did he change?

The Three Steps of Change

There are three steps of change:

1. You have a *moment of enlightenment.*

2. You make a *decision* to take a different course of action from what you have been doing.

3. Commitment to your decision leads to *sustained action*, which brings about permanent change.

Joshua Chamberlain went through these three steps en route to becoming one of the greatest leaders of the Civil War. Let's look at both the fundamental character and situational changes for him:

FUNDAMENTAL CHARACTER CHANGE:

<u>Moment of Enlightenment</u>: When war broke out, as an avowed abolitionist and Federalist, Chamberlain realized he had to take action in support of his beliefs.

<u>Decision</u>: Instead of going to Europe as he was supposed to, he enlisted.

<u>Sustained Action</u>: Realizing he didn't have the expertise to command right away, he apprenticed himself to a more experienced officer, learning the skills needed to command.

Situational change:

<u>Moment of Enlightenment</u>: Realizing the 20th Maine was going to be over-run, he also knew that the attacking forces had to be as exhausted and on the brink of collapse as his own men.

<u>Decision</u>: He gave the order to charge when most other officers would have given the order to retreat.

<u>Sustained Action</u>: Chamberlain personally led the charge, making sure they defeated not only the Confederates who were in the assault, but also straightened out the Union line for a better defensive position.

Moment of Enlightenment.

Most of what you do day-in and day-out is habit. And habits are extremely difficult to change. To have a moment of enlightenment you have to become open-minded, one of the character traits we've already talked about. You have to be able to change your point of view—your perspective. You must get out of your every-day rut.

Break out of your comfort zone and look at something in the opposite way you've always looked at it. Entertain the possibility that what you think is your greatest strength, might actually be a defense (a blind spot) layered over your greatest flaw that can blind you to opportunities to change. Reverse thinking is a very strong tool to help find moments of enlightenment.

An Example

A simple moment of enlightenment for me came in the Special Forces Qualification course. During a patrolling exercise, we spent several February days being rained on—not exactly the most comfortable experience. Several students had to be medevacked out for hypothermia. When the exercise concluded, we were given an eight-hour break, still out in the middle of the woods, before moving on to the next training exercise. We no longer had to be on alert.

It was still pouring and cold. Most students huddled, shivering and sopping wet, underneath their ponchos. I watched, though, as one student ignored the elements and walked about, gathering firewood. He piled it up, and then worked hard to get a fire started. After quite a bit of effort, he had a roaring blaze and a grateful circle of students standing around, warming themselves and drying off.

My moment of enlightenment? When miserable, don't just hunker down and ignore the environment—instead, take action to make the situation better. Over the years since, that simple realization has served me well in numerous situations. Thinking about being warm and dry while wet and cold did nothing. A decision was required, followed by a course of action—in this example, literally going against the elements.

Ways to Have Moments of Enlightenment

Moments of enlightenment come in several ways:

- A new experience you've never encountered before affects you.
- Something you've experienced before affects you in a new way.
- You witness someone else doing something differently, and it affects you.

A successful person is always looking at the world around him, trying to uncover previously unseen possibilities. The more information you gather, the more possible courses of action you have.

Many times, those who surround us are trying to give us the gift of enlightenment, but we ignore their message. In a marriage, often one partner is trying to give the spouse enlightenment, but the message is ignored. At work, a co-worker might be pointing something out to you, which goes by without notice. Sometimes, if you just listen to *yourself*, you're subconsciously trying to give yourself a MOE. When you finish this book, you'll be directed to go back and re-read the answers you've written down for the exercises. Read them with an open mind and see what you're *really* saying in your answers.

Take the Challenge: Exercise 19
**Fold a piece of paper in thirds. On the left third, write
down three Moments of Enlightenment you've had since
beginning this book.**

Make a decision

Your moment of enlightenment is internal. So is the decision you must make next. If you don't make a decision to change, your moment of enlightenment will be gone—worthless.

In Area One, you learned that decisions involve a succinct statement of what it is you want to achieve. It's important to write your decision—your goal—down. This is the first external action in the process of change.

<u>Take the Challenge: Exercise 20</u>
Using the paper from exercise 19, in the middle column, write down a decision to change for each of the three Moments of Enlightenment.

Chart a sustained course of action.

Don't expect immediate, burning-bush change as soon as you've made your decision. While this does happen, it is very, very rare. Change is a slow process that requires dedication and commitment and most of all Sustained Action.

I've had varied teaching experiences: Special Forces team, JFK Special Warfare Center, Masters Degree in Education, Martial Arts teaching, writing teacher, universities, conferences, organizational speaker, etc. I can't count the number of times I heard someone say: "I always wanted to write a book, but . . ." "I always wanted to get a black belt, but . . ." "I was going to try out for Special Forces, but . . ."

The successful don't do buts. The successful are not wanna-be's. They learn. They decide. They act. They sustain the action.

Train For Change

The military is very big on training because it wants to change people from civilians into soldiers. The goal of Special Forces training is to change regular soldiers into elite warriors. You can use some of the Special Forces training templates to achieve sustained change in your life.

The history of Special Forces Assessment and Selection (SFAS) goes back to the formation of Delta Force, and before that back to the British SAS. SFAS was created in an attempt to learn from history and others who'd already done what Special Forces needed to do.

According to official doctrine, SFAS tests an applicant's tactical skills, leadership, physical fitness, motivation and ability to cope with stress. This is done through over-land movements, psychological tests, physical fitness tests, swim test, runs, obstacle courses, small unit tactics exercises, land navigation exercises and individual and team problem solving.

Aspiring Special Forces soldiers coming to the course are advised that their mind is their best weapon. That being physically fit isn't enough to get them through. Applicants should be prepared for anything.

In this type of training, expectations are unclear. There are unknown variables and standards. This places students under stress—as you've already learned, an excellent evaluation technique to see if someone can be successful. I've seen students become so frustrated that they quit.

There's none of the harassment or 'false' stress that's used in many training situations. Once you've been through a 'getting screamed in your face' training environment, the second time you experience it, the effect is almost ludicrous. When you are testing the elite the stress has to be real.

Focus on the times in your life when the stress was real and examine your actions.

Goal-aligned Training Programs

Just as your goals must be aligned to support one another, your training plans must be goal-aligned. Often you have many things you want to achieve. You must prioritize your goals, both primary and subordinate—again, in writing. When designing your personal training programs, this priority must be clearly understood, so your time is well spent and your training for one goal doesn't become counter-productive to another.

Goal-alignment must happen every day. As a writer, when I start a new book, I post my one sentence original idea on my desk and read it every day to keep myself on task and avoid going off on tangents.

As a martial arts student and then instructor, I learned that the key to success, as is the case in many other training fields, is repetition. You have to do the same kick again and again and again—correctly—until one day, after thousands and thousands of kicks, the motion becomes instinctual. Sustained action changes habits.

In Ranger school, the proper response to an ambush is drilled into students day after day—because it goes against your survival instinct to charge into an attacking force. Repetition is the key to both training, as well as training for the right goal at the right time. Follow your goal-aligned training plan every day—do it right every day—and sooner or later you will achieve a new habit to replace the one you want to change.

Scientists have found that while you can't 'unprogram' neural pathways that are your habits, you can build 'detours' around bad habits by building parallel neural pathways. The more you sustain the new habit, the stronger that pathway becomes, and the less power the old habit holds.

Take the Challenge: Exercise 21

For each decision to change you listed in Exercise 20, in the right column, define the sustained action you would have to do to achieve the change you desire.

Focus Your Training Program On Yourself, Not Other People.

If you've read this far into the Green Beret Guide, you're searching for something. You want to change things in your life. One of the most dangerous phases in change is when you realize you're not where you want to be, but then look outward for the reasons—looking for someone or something else to be at fault. This is especially true in relationships, where we tend to think changing the other person will improve the relationship.

The only person you can change is yourself. Trying to change another person will often bring about more negative results than positive. Learn from those who have something you want. Ask for help when you need it. Try to be open to that which at first doesn't seem to make sense or fit. A successful individual focuses on changing himself—which is a very long-term process.

Training is action. Doing. Not talking about doing. The bottom line comes down to doing the hard work of sustained action, and rigorously evaluating your results.

Some of the hardest courses in the military involve no harassment, no screaming, no yelling. Elite courses stay focused on achieving set standards. When I led my team through Danish Scout Swim School, we were told on the first day what was required to graduate:

- Swim thirty meters underwater.
- Free dive ten meters down.
- Do a ten-kilometer surface swim within a certain time.
- Do a one-kilometer surface swim within a certain time.
- Successfully complete the school's obstacle course.
- Tie three knots around a pipe while submerged.

Then we spent several weeks practicing these events along with other training. The instructors told us what to do each day, and we did it. And it was very, very hard.

Set your evaluation standards the same way you set goals—use one sentence, and write them down. Then do it. Day after day.

<u>Take the Challenge: Exercise 22</u>
Using your goal-aligned training program from Exercises
19-21, list the standards you need to achieve to sustain
change. Post these standards where you can see them
every day. Make the standards external goals that can
clearly be assessed—you either achieve the standard, or
you don't.

Change: The Artist's Imagination

95% of the students I've worked with as a writing instructor
have not really improved as writers. Perhaps it reflects on
my abilities as a teacher. But I also found 95% of the
students I worked with as a martial arts instructor did not
reach Black Belt level. As a teacher at the JFK Special
Warfare Center & School the success rate was somewhat
higher, about 30%, but these were highly motivated volunteers who'd already been through several screening
processes.

It's reported that eighty-two percent of Americans
believe they can write a book. The actual number that actually start writing a book is much lower. The percentage that

manage to produce a completed manuscript is far lower, down in the single digits.

Whatever you want to achieve, whatever you want to be, the only solution is to actually do it—by taking action every day to get one step closer to your goal.

In writing, I learned that this was called 'bum glue'— gluing my bum to a chair every day, sitting at the computer, and actually writing. All my great dreams, my wonderful thoughts, all of that was worthless if I didn't sit down and actually put words on page.

A writer by definition must write. Whatever it is you want to achieve must be externalized into action, not left to thought where it will wither way until it's worthless.

To be successful, change must become a way of life.

TOOL SIX: HOW DO YOU BUILD THE COURAGE TO CHANGE?

There are several definitions of courage:

- *The state or quality of mind or spirit that enables one to face danger with self-possession, confidence, and resolution.*
- *The ability to do something that frightens one. Strength in the face of pain or grief.*

The dictionary also tells us that fear is a feeling of alarm or disquiet caused by the expectation of danger, pain, disaster, etc. Since courage is taking action in the face of fear, this means you must:

1. Accept that your fears are part of your character.
2. Understand what you really fear—often your **blind spot**-- is something you are often unaware of, but have begun to look at after Tool 4.
3. Determine what actions you must take to

overcome your fear in your decision making, rather than ignoring it.

4. Train to overcome fear through sustained action.
5. Prepare for the things you fear the worst in order to reduce the fear.

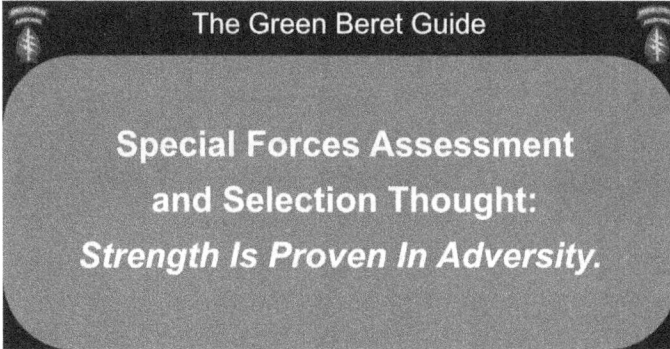

The Green Beret Guide

Special Forces Assessment and Selection Thought:
Strength Is Proven In Adversity.

Blood Lesson: The Men Who Did

Heroism is acting in the face of fear.

The Problem

On Sunday, 3 September 1993, a Blackhawk helicopter was shot down in Mogadishu, Somalia. An armed mob was closing on the downed helicopter and its crew. The only American forces in the vicinity were two elite Delta Force Operatives flying overheard in another chopper.

The Solution

Sergeants Shughart and Gordon requested permission to secure and rescue the men from the downed Blackhawk. Being professional soldiers and having watched the situation unfold, they knew that the grounded soldiers had slim odds of holding off that mob until additional help arrived.

The sergeants repeatedly volunteered for a mission no one had ordered them to do, in a country none of them had any stake in. To rescue men they weren't even sure were alive and did not personally know. On a mission dictated from half a world away, with nebulous goals that were constantly changing at the National Command Authority level.

In the same situation, an ordinary person would not have made such a request. And when the request was granted, wouldn't have jumped from the hovering helicopter, knowing the advancing mob was getting closer.

But these sergeants were not ordinary people— Sergeants Shughart and Gordon were Special Operations Forces. They were the elite. Being courageous in the face of fear was their state of mind.

Why did they do this? How were their actions different from the way most others would have reacted? What made them elite?

Here is the Medal of Honor citation for Master Sergeant Gordon:

Rank and organization: Master Sergeant, U.S. Army. Place and date: 3 October 1993, Mogadishu, Somalia. Entered service at:-----Born: Lincoln, Maine. Citation: Master Sergeant Gordon, United States Army, distinguished himself by actions above and beyond the call of duty on 3 October 1993, while serving as Sniper Team Leader, United States Army Special Operations Command with Task Force Ranger in Mogadishu, Somalia.

Master Sergeant Gordon's sniper team provided precision fires from the lead helicopter during an assault and at two helicopter crash sites, while subjected to intense automatic weapons and rocket propelled grenade fires. When Master Sergeant Gordon learned that ground forces were not immediately available to secure the second crash site, he and another sniper unhesitatingly volunteered to be inserted to protect the four critically wounded personnel, despite being well aware of the growing number of enemy personnel closing in on the site.

After his third request to be inserted, Master Sergeant Gordon received permission to perform his volunteer mission. When debris and enemy ground fires at the site caused them to abort the first attempt, Master Sergeant Gordon was inserted one hundred meters south of the crash site.

Equipped with only his sniper rifle and a pistol, Master Sergeant Gordon and his fellow sniper, while under intense small arms fire from the enemy, fought their way through a dense maze of shanties and shacks to reach the critically injured crew members. Master Sergeant Gordon immediately pulled the pilot and the other crew members from the aircraft, establishing a perimeter which placed him and his fellow sniper in the most vulnerable position. Master Sergeant Gordon used his long range rifle and side arm to kill an undetermined number of attackers until he depleted his ammunition. Master Sergeant Gordon then went back to the wreckage, recovering some of the crew's weapons and ammunition.

Despite the fact that he was critically low on ammunition, he provided some of it to the dazed pilot and then radioed for help. Master Sergeant Gordon continued to travel the perimeter, protecting the downed crew. After his team member was fatally wounded and his own rifle ammunition exhausted, Master Sergeant Gordon returned to the wreckage, recovering a rifle with the last five rounds of ammunition and gave it to the pilot with the words, "good luck." Then, armed only with his pistol, Master Sergeant Gordon continued to fight until he was fatally wounded.

His actions saved the pilot's life. Master Sergeant Gordon's extraordinary heroism and devotion to duty were in keeping with *the highest standards of military service and reflect great credit upon him, his unit and the United States Army.*

The Lesson

Shughart and Gordon were heroes. They took an action to help their comrades, despite their fear. The sergeants were able take the action, because they had the necessary character and training. Because they had a primary motivator that allowed them to overcome their fear. While this is another extreme example, the things you face in your life are important to you. There are many events which will cause you to dig deep and find the courage to face.

Fear and Your Blind Spot

We all have a 'blind spot', a part of our personality that is hidden from ourselves. Often, it is this blind spot that keeps us from being successful. And the majority of the time this blind spot is rooted in our deepest fears.

It is critical to find your blind spots and the first step in that is to be ...

Honesty with Self

Honesty plays a key role in being successful. The only way to uncover your blind spot is to be honest with yourself, and honest with those who want to help you. It is amazing that often people pay large amounts of money to see a therapist, walk into the session, and then lie, defeating the entire purpose of what they are paying for.

In the beginning of this book, in exercise 1, I asked you to write down what you feared the most. Odds are, your blind spot is affiliated with that fear somehow. However, your defenses are so good, that often your blind spot is the exact opposite of what you'd describe as your greatest strength. Sometimes it could even be what you view as your greatest strength, because it might actually be your greatest defense and thus very powerful.

There are tools to help you understand your character and fears, and to learn to be courageous as you face them. We already discussed looking at the opposite character traits found in your Myers-Briggs Character type. Another way is to examine your strengths and see where the potential blind spot might be uses the . . .

Traits, Needs, Flaws Paradigm

This paradigm takes a character trait, defines the need associated with it, and illustrates the potential flaw you'll face dealing with that part of your character.

Every character trait is double-edged: there is both a positive and a negative potential. A good way to delve deeper into your blind spot, to understand your true nature, is to look at what you consider your character strengths—then find the need driving that strength, and then the corresponding weakness or flaw you are less comfortable looking at when you push that need to an extreme.

For example, consider these character traits, needs and corresponding character flaws (blind spots):

TRAIT	NEED	FLAW
Loyal	To be trusted	Gullible
Adventurous	To have change	Unreliable
Altruistic	To be loved	Submissive
Tolerant	To have no conflict	No conviction
Decisive	To be in charge	Impetuous
Realistic	To be balanced	Outer control
Competitive	To achieve goals	Overlook cost
Idealistic	To be the best	Naive

Take the Challenge: Exercise 23

In one word, record what you believe to be your greatest
character trait. (the list above is only a suggested one)

Take the Challenge: Exercise 24
Using that trait, write down the corresponding need and potential flaw (blind spot).

Everyone wants to succeed, but most people succumb to the enemy—fear:

- Fear of failure
- Fear of lack of security
- Fear of success—which can be the most insidious and hardest fear to identify

Most fear is subconscious. Fear is a fact of life, but it can become debilitating, if not faced and dealt with before a triggering crisis is faced. It is likely at the core of most of the day-to-day problems you face.

For example, in uncertain times, when business is bad and lay-offs threaten, a tremendous amount of work force energy can go into employees worrying about job security—rather than accomplishing their team's mission. This can lead to a negative spiral of defeat and failure. There is such a thing as a self-fulfilling prophecy. When fear becomes too great, the emotion itself can bring about what is feared.

When you begin to panic, it expends energy that should be used to avert whatever it is that you fear. Are you willing to let the hidden enemy predetermine your goal's failure or success.

<u>Take the Challenge: Exercise 25</u>
Describe the last time you wanted to do something you knew was the right thing to do, but you didn't do it. What kept you from doing it?

While your answer might be something mundane such as laziness, no time, wasn't important enough, etc., peel away those reasons and search for the fear underneath.

It's not uncommon to design your life based on your hidden fears (blind spots), creating your own bunker—more of a cave to hide in, than a courageous place from which to succeed at your goals.

If fear prevents you from committing to achieving your goals, your failure is ensured by your own hand—a self-fulfilling prophecy.

<u>Take the Challenge: Exercise 26</u>
Based on what you've uncovered in this Tool and under Character, list those traits, needs and flaws that you feel compromise your character. Then list the fears (blinds spots) that you suspect hurt you.

Fear is not a total negative. Two of the primary reasons why this emotion exists—that you can use to your advantage—are to serve as a warning (when you're in danger) and an indicator (sometimes, of exactly what you need to do).

FEAR As A Warning

We fear things because we believe they are threats to us. And sometimes things *do* threaten us. So to toss fear on the scrap heap opens us up to getting hurt—not the same thing as the pain that can come with positive change.

You've heard people talk about sixth sense. I believe sixth sense is the power of the subconscious taking care of us. A part of our mind that combines signals from the five senses, and warns us when something we don't consciously see, touch, smell, taste or hear is a real threat.

A point man on a military patrol should have excellent

sixth sense. For example, a good point man's eyes might notice something—a broken twig, a trip wire—that his mind doesn't consciously process. But his subconscious, which is also processing information, sends a warning to the conscious mind in the form of the emotion of fear. Of course, he must be tuned into his indicators to recognize the trigger, and act on the basis of his fear.

You should pay attention to vague feelings of unease or fear. Don't ignore these feelings. Because sometimes they are indications of real trouble. If you get 'bad vibes' from a person or a situation, focus on it. This is part of developing your elite character traits.

A company in Los Angeles (Gavin de Becker and *The Gift of Fear*) that consults with movie stars about stalkers and other dangers, advises their clients to pay attention to vague feelings of unease or fear. To not ignore these feelings. Because sometimes they are indications of real trouble coming. If you get 'bad vibes' from a person or a situation focus on it. After something bad has happened to you, how many times do you look back and realize there were warning signs that you ignored?

After something bad has happened to you, how many times do you look back and realize there were warning signs that you ignored?

Take the Challenge: Exercise 27

Think back to the last really bad thing that happened to you. Write it down. Then write down the warning signs that were present before it happened, but that you didn't focus on.

These warning signs are fear indicators that you should write down and post so that you can see them every day.

Read them, focus on them, and examine if they are coming up again with regard to something else in your life.

Just like your anger *flash points* tell you something about yourself, your fear *indicators* are important character traits to learn. The wall of fear is the demarcation line between being ordinary and successful. The ordinary person lives a life filled with fear, and cut off from positive action because of it. The successful person has fear, but acts toward their desired goals in spite of it, constantly pushing their wall of courage further outward.

Fear can often indicate exactly what you need to do in order to succeed and the direction in which you need to push your courage. Yes, the fear is a warning that you could fail. But remember--if you don't try, you can never succeed.

And you'll never know your true fear threshold, if you're not willing to challenge it.

Expand Your Comfort Zone by Venturing into Your Courage Zone

The best way to overcome fear is to prepare for it. To train for it. You have a comfort zone and around that you have a courage zone. Most people rarely venture into their courage zone because of fear. The successful person ventures into their courage zone often. By doing so, you expand your comfort zone and push the boundaries of both your comfort and courage zones further and further—this is conquering fear and becoming successful.

We cannot think ourselves through change; we must make the decision to start change. Then, take action. No one ever got a Medal of Honor for thinking about doing something heroic. Training is repetitive action. It is the key to over-coming fear because it builds your confidence. We talked about this in the previous Tool: Change.

The number of airborne qualified soldiers in the army far exceeds the number of airborne slots. Why does the army send so many more people, particularly officers, through airborne training than it needs?

At the introduction to ground week, the first of three distinct phases of training, you're told that it's not normal to jump out of a perfectly functioning airplane. In fact, it goes against a person's ingrained survival instincts. And when survival is threatened, the normal reaction is fear.

Short of actually shooting at trainees, airborne school is one of the army's ways to put a large number of soldiers in a high-stress situation and make them take an action directly into the face of the fear—throwing themselves out of an airplane door at fifteen hundred feet. To be successful, you must face fear. You must train to act in a positive, targeted manner in the face of it, moving you closer to achieving your goals.

I'm not just talking about physical conflict. Mental stress can take a significant toll. In West Point's Beast Barracks, physical hazing is prohibited. Yet plebes are under stress the entire time, due to mental pressure and the requirement to perform, to act, despite it. Train for fear, by regularly performing under pressure. You don't really know someone until you see them act in a crisis. Don't wait until a real crisis to know your reaction to the unexpected.

In Ranger school, the proper response to an ambush is drilled into students day after day, because as noted earlier, it goes against your instinct to charge *into* an ambush. Repetition is the key to this. Do it right every day and sooner or later it will become the right habit, usually replacing a bad one.

In the US Army Ranger School you're taught to do things you wouldn't normally do. One thing you are trained to deal with is getting ambushed.

Your patrol is walking along a trail and suddenly you are fired upon from the right. Your fear wants you to jump in the convenient ditch to the left—to avoid the ambush.

However, if the ambush is set up correctly—that ditch is mined and YOU'LL DIE if you do that.

In life, avoiding problems by running from them doesn't solve the problem.

Your next fear-driven instinct is to just hit the ground. Stay where you're at and do nothing. Except you're in the kill zone and if you stay there, well, YOU'LL GET KILLED.

We all want to ignore problems. Because that's the inherent nature of a problem. But ignoring your greatest problem will keep you in the kill zone and the result is inevitable.

The third thing you want to do is run forward or back on the trail to get out of the kill zone-- escape.

Except, if the ambush is done right, the heaviest weapons are firing on either end of the kill zone. And YOU'LL DIE.

We want to avoid problems by going back to the past or imaging it will get better in the future even if we don't change anything.

The correct solution is the hardest choice because it requires courage: you must conquer your fear, turn right and assault into the ambushing force. It is the best way to not only survive, but WIN. To tackle problems, you must face them.

How do you expand your Comfort Zone?

Do something POSITIVE you don't want to do—something that expands your Comfort Zone by repeatedly going into your Courage Zone:

- If you're typically introverted, make yourself approach and talk to a complete stranger every day.
- If you're a practical person, force yourself to make a minor decision intuitively.
- Have you ever spent a night by yourself outdoors?
- Have you ever sat still for just one hour doing nothing—no TV, no music, no book. Just by yourself? Looking inward?

Practice facing your blinds spots, regularly acting to achieve the goals your hidden fears are blocking.

Take the Challenge: Exercise 28
Based on your answer to Exercise 26, pick one flaw and write down one positive act that would challenge you to face that blind spot, act in the face of fear and enter your courage zone?

Take the Challenge: Exercise 29
For the next week, do this one positive act every day. By

**the end of the week, your Comfort Zone will have
increased.**

Disaster Planning to Reduce Fear and Increase Success

A technique we used in Special Forces was to do worst-case
scenarios and plan for dealing with potential disasters.
There were two major reasons for this. First, to actually plan
for the worst case since it usually involved our lives being on
the line. But secondly, planning for dealing with disaster
actually reduces fear and allows you to focus more of your
energy on positive success, instead of worrying about "what
if things go wrong?" because you've already answered the
question in your disaster planning.

Disasters rarely happen in isolation. In my series of
books *The Green Beret Guide to Seven Great Disasters*, I show
the Rule of Seven, which shows how it takes seven cascade
events to lead up to a disaster.

Take any situation you might face and worst case it.
What will you do if that worst case happens? If you don't
have a plan already in place, you need to make one. Because
your subconscious knows you don't have a plan and it keeps
you in a constant state of tension and worry, sapping the
strength you need to be successful.

<u>Take the Challenge: Exercise 30</u>
Fold a piece of paper in half, and on the left side, for the following areas, write down a potential catastrophe that could occur:
Physical:
Financial:
Natural disaster:
Work:
Relationship:
The next major task you have to do:

For example, look at where you live. Are you in a hurricane zone? An earthquake zone? A tsunami zone? Forest fire area? Do you have a plan already in place and prepared to be executed in case the worst happens? If you live in a house that is below sea level in a city that relies on levees to keep the sea at bay, do you have a plan in place in case the levees fail? If you live in a hurricane area, do you have your important papers, pictures, keepsakes, food, supplies, etc. already packed and ready to be loaded? Do you have spare gas cans filled up and ready to be taken? Do you never let your gas tank get below half? Do you have a checklist you can refer to in case of evacuation so you don't forget to do something important, like turn the gas off? You need a 'go bag'. The website USA.gov will give you links to your local area/government if you type 'go bag' in the search. For more detail see The Green Beret Preparation and Survival Guide or check out free, downloadable slideshows on all aspects of preparation.

It's too late to make these plans once the catastrophe occurs.

Take the Challenge: Exercise 31
On the right side of the paper from exercise 30, write out your plan in case the catastrophe occurs and then make the necessary preparations.

Courage: The Artist's Imagination

As a writer, I've learned to trust my subconscious. I warn new writers not to edit themselves too harshly while writing a novel—their subconscious will put things into the manuscript that they won't consciously recognize the immediate need for, but will serve an important purpose later on. I teach writers to trust that the part of their mind they don't consciously control is working for them, planting seeds that will be reaped later on.

In the same way, paying attention to fears in your life that don't make much sense now, facing them with courage and training to deal with your indicators, will pay off in huge dividends later.

Writing fiction is an extremely precarious occupation in terms of security. I advise new writers to catastrophe plan—have a back-up plan in case it doesn't work out. Not because I don't think it will work out for them, but so they don't waste their creative energy worrying and focus on their writing. Writers who constantly live in fear of not getting the next book contract eventually break down—and don't get another contract.

Courage is a state of mind.

Courage is acknowledging fear, then taking action in the face of it. The more you do this, the more success you will achieve.

AREA TWO CONCLUSION:
WHO, THE GREEN BERET GUIDE

The tools in this book help you change the way you're living. A key to the Circle of Success is understanding yourself, particularly your blind spot. Uncovering the hidden fears that keep you mired in the mundane. Then making decisions to act and train to be the successful you.

Change is a long-term, three-step process ultimately requiring sustained action. But in the long run, trying to achieve your goals without understanding yourself and factoring in your fears, is counter-productive.

A classic example of training that is counter-productive to mission accomplishment occurred during my plebe year at West Point. The Academy is designed to train leaders for the modern army. Yet while I was there, some training was still rooted in archaic techniques. Plebes were expected to memorize large amounts of plebe 'knowledge'. One of these was General Schofield's definition of discipline:

"The discipline which makes the soldiers of a free country reliable in battle is not to be gained by harsh or tyrannical treatment. On the contrary, such treatment is far more likely to destroy than to make an army." General Schofield.

I remember standing in the hallway of the barracks at West Point, braced against the wall by an upperclassman, who would demand I recite the definition as a form a hazing. There was an inherent contradiction between the content of what I was saying and the context under which I was saying it. Did this training result in daring, sustained change? Not compared to what I learned among the successful in Special Forces.

Blood Lesson: From Regular Soldier to Guerilla Leader

The Problem

In 1941, Colonel Russell Volckman, a 1934 West Point graduate, was serving in the Philippines. At that time, an assignment to the Philippines was considered a plum posting. The exotic locale, low cost of living and working under General Douglas MacArthur were all strong attractions to young graduates. The US Army was still in World War I-mode—it is said every army is always prepared to fight the last war, not the next one because they aren't willing to change.

When the Japanese invaded the Philippines, Volckman and many other Americans were captured as the last stronghold on Bataan Peninsula fell.

The Solution

Volckman did not accept his fate as a prisoner. The night before what was to become known at the Bataan Death March began, he and several other soldiers slipped under the wire and escaped into the jungle.

While General MacArthur snuck out of Bataan on a PT Boat, vowing "I will return", Volckman later wrote a book titled *We Remained*.

Volckman had no experience in unconventional warfare. If he had followed orders, he would have stayed a prisoner and gone on the Death March. If he had survived that, he would have spent the rest of the war imprisoned under horrible conditions.

His character was such, though, that he disobeyed orders and escaped. Then he began to learn a new way of fighting—linking up with indigenous forces. Along with the others who escaped with him, they began a guerilla warfare campaign against the Japanese that would last over three years.

Volckman had the courage to violate his order to surrender (Rule breaking—Tool 9) and then to survive behind enemy lines for three years. Not just survive, but to learn how to conduct a style of warfare for which he'd had little training. He learned day-to-day, on the job.

He had a Moment of Enlightenment, made a Decision and conducted Sustained Action for three years. He displayed courage in the face of harsh conditions, day after day.

The Result

The guerilla forces in the Philippines became so effective, they tied down large parts of the Japanese Army. These behind-the-lines fighters caused tremendous problems for the Japanese and helped insure the success of the invasion, when MacArthur finally did return in 1944.

After World War II, Volckman along with Colonel Aaron Banks, fought to establish a force that would be prepared to fight the next war behind the lines. When Volckman and Banks finally received the approval to establish a "special" unit that would conduct unconventional warfare—the beginning of Special Forces—they faced a daunting task.

How would they select and assess the solders who would be part of the unit? What kind of character should Special Forces soldiers have? They focused on those men who had expertise in guerilla warfare, spoke foreign languages, and were independent thinkers who could operate on their own, as well as members of a team.

Then Banks devised a Special Forces training program, drawing on his and others like Volckman's experiences, to teach Special Forces soldiers their Blood Lessons. A training plan for teaching a soldier how to conquer fear was designed with very high standards for success.

Align Character, Change and Courage—to Win!

You're now ready to pull together everything you've learned about *what, why, where, character, change* and *courage*. In the conclusion of *Area 1: Wins*, I gave you my A-Team experience, and I've shared many other military examples and templates since. But as you've learned, *Area 2: Who*—and change—is all about you.

So, in this area's conclusion, I'm giving you a very important challenge:

To review the Circle of Success again and again—based on the work you've done so far and the work you've yet to do in *Area 3: Dares*—and then again, if needed. To keep reviewing and learning and changing your goals and decisions and training programs. To continue challenging yourself to be successful and to learn and to grow, as you master the tools of digging deeper into what you need and what you want and how you want to get it.

Let's take a look at what you've accomplished so far:

- You've recorded WHAT you want to change and achieve. You've written these goals down, so you can track your progress and refine your intent as you learn and grow.
- You've recorded WHY you want to achieve those goals.
- You've studied WHERE you will be achieving those goals and how achieving that goal will interact with your environment.
- You've examined your CHARACTER, both your strengths and flaws. You've recorded the fears and blind spots that keep you from achieving your goals.
- You are using the three steps to CHANGE.
- You are utilizing COURAGE to act in the face of fear and expand your courage zone.

Now, it's time take all you've learned and make these parts of the Circle of Success a way of life.

Your life.

It's time to read *Area 3: Dares*, to claim the successful life for your own.

AREA THREE: DARES

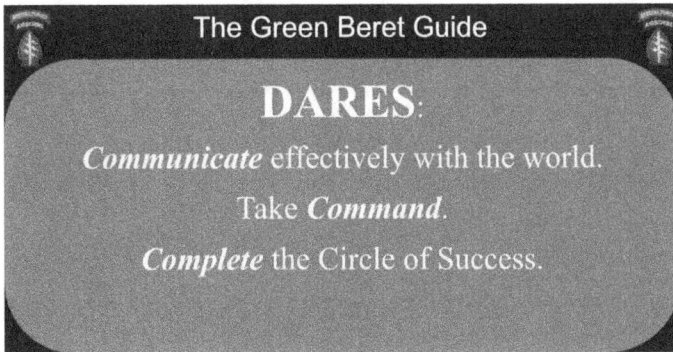

The Green Beret Guide

DARES:

Communicate effectively with the world.

Take *Command*.

Complete the Circle of Success.

In *Area Two*, you created a plan for change. Use the tools in this section to look deep into yourself and discover what you want to change, so you can achieve your *Area One* goals.

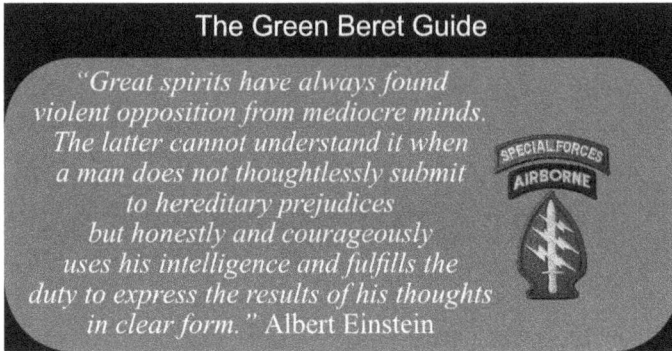

The Green Beret Guide

"Great spirits have always found violent opposition from mediocre minds. The latter cannot understand it when a man does not thoughtlessly submit to hereditary prejudices but honestly and courageously uses his intelligence and fulfills the duty to express the results of his thoughts in clear form." Albert Einstein

What you've been learning up to now is the basics of the Green Beret Guide. The craft. Now, it's time to graduate from learning craft to being an artist. It's time separate from the norm, break rules and *Dare* to be different.

To succeed at being different, it is critical to have effective Communication, master a Command of self, and do a Complete integration of all tools.

Because Special Forces are primarily teachers, effective Communication skills are valued. Personal Command is a core Special Forces trait. Every individual is expected to take charge and use their initiative.

Integration of these tools into your life takes you to another level, where you are then able to go back and refine your answers to the exercises in each of the various tools, making greater change and improving your way of life.

TOOL SEVEN: COMMUNICATE
EFFECTIVELY WITH THE WORLD

T he successful communicate clearly and effectively, so they can evoke a desired response and achieve their goals among others—family, co-workers and friends.

Communication is essential to success: it is a large part of the way you interact with other people. It is a two-way street: you have to get your message across to others, and receive the *true* messages others are sending.

The goal in communication is to be succinct, to the point, and *evoke a response.*

The Green Beret Guide

**Special Forces Assessment
and Selection Thought:
*Defeat isn't bitter if
you don't swallow it.***

Blood Lesson: When Can Their Glory Fade?

Miscommunication in battle gets people killed. A classic example of this is a military operation made famous by a poem written by Tennyson: The Charge of the Light Brigade at Balaclava.

Without delving into the backstory explaining why the British were battling the Russians in the Crimea, suffice it to say at a certain point in this war, the British found themselves facing the Russians at the Battle of Balaclava.

The Problem

Lord Raglan, the commander of British Army Forces, sent a written order to the cavalry:

"Lord Raglan wishes the cavalry to advance rapidly to the front and to prevent the enemy carrying away the guns. Horse Artillery may accompany. French cavalry is on your left. Immediate."

"Attack what?" the cavalry commander asked the bearer.

The courier gestured vaguely. *"There, my Lord, is your enemy."*

The only guns the cavalry commander could see from his position were at the very end of the valley, over a mile away. And thus the fate of the Light Brigade was sealed.

In response to the order, the Earl of Cardigan led six-hundred and seventy-three men straight into the valley between the Fediukhine Heights and the Causeway Heights. The Russians controlled not only the end of the valley toward which they were riding, but the heights on both sides. The Russians had over fifty artillery pieces and twenty battalions of Infantry massed around this pocket of death. It was over a mile from the mouth of the valley to the Russian guns at the end which Cardigan thought were his objective and led his men.

As they galloped forward, the courier officer, realizing that the Light Brigade was heading down the valley instead of toward the closer Causeway Heights, which was the true objective, dashed forward on his horse, wildly waving his sword. He was trying to let Cardigan know that they were going toward the wrong objective (albeit a bit late). However, as fate often has it, once things started going bad, they went from bad to worse.

The courier was struck by a fragment of a shell that killed him instantly. His sword fell from his hand, but his arm remained erect and the death grip of his knees kept him in the saddle. He galloped through the advancing Light Brigade, his true message dead with him.

The Russian artillery began to fire in earnest. Gaps opened in the Light Brigade lines as shot and shell swept through them. But they never paused, nor stopped. The Russian infantry also began to fire, adding to the carnage. Still the Light Brigade charged on.

The survivors did reach the end of the valley and swept over the guns. So stunning was this attack that the Russian cavalry behind the guns, even though they far outnumbered the survivors of the Light Brigade, turned and ran despite the pleas of their officers.

However, the survivors among the Russian artillerymen manning the over-run guns, began to fire again. The Russian cavalry regrouped and advanced, and all the Light Brigade could do now was retreat. There was no support from the rest of the British, because no one in the British lines knew what they had done, since it wasn't what they had been ordered to.

The Solution

Wasn't very pretty. When the smoke cleared, there were only one-hundred and ninety-five men left. The stupidity combined with reckless bravery caused a French Marshall to proclaim:

"*It is magnificent, but it is not war.*"

On the Russian side, the commanders could only conclude that the British had been drunk.

> "*When can their glory fade?*
> *O the wild charge they made!*
> *All the world wonder'd.*
> *Honor the charge they made!*
> *Honor the Light Brigade,*
> *Noble six hundred!*"
> Tennyson

Nice poem.
Bad written order.

The Lesson

Write with your reader in mind and what response is desired.

Raglan, when he scribbled out his order, knew where he wanted the Light Brigade to attack. But since his point of view was different than Cardigan's, literally, he failed to specify the position—he failed to take into account the perspective of the recipient of the order, who was in the lower ground of the valley and could not see the true objective.

What Is Communication?

Communication is the means by which we exchange both information and emotion. It bridges the gap between inner thoughts and feelings and the external world. A successful person does not exist in a vacuum. Excellent communication is an essential skill. Communication is a two-way activity. Too many people focus on their ability to send a message, and ignore their capability to receive information and emotion in return.

When people communicate something that bothers you, focus on what was really communicated. You're having an emotional reaction because something that was communicated, either verbally or non-verbally, resonated inside you. Fear plays a role in communication—we often fear being honest and react negatively to honesty from others.

Psychologists say only a small percentage of oral communication is the actual words. Most information is transmitted through non-verbal cues. In the same manner the phrase 'read between the lines' is a critical one when dealing with written communication.

There are two primary forms of communication: written and oral. Another type of communication we've have already discussed, although you might not have seen it that way, is action. We communicate very strongly through the actions we do.

Communication, in any form, is the key to interacting with other people.

Written Communication

In my experience as a novelist, and having taught writing for three decades, I've found that approximately ninety-five percent of the people I've worked with don't communicate adequately with the written word. Note that we're once more back to that magic number of five percent.

I don't say this because the people I've worked with are incapable of written communication. They fail because they already think they *are* capable but are not willing to learn the craft of writing. They have a fixed mindset, not a growth one. Becoming a successful writer, like becoming successful at anything else, is a skill that can be learned.

Think like your reader

The key to good written communication is to not think like the writer, but to think like the reader.

The message in your head will be lost if you cannot express it well in writing. To make it important, the correct message has to develop in your reader's head. The Charge of the Light Brigade couldn't have illustrated this better, or more poignantly. You must make the reader's point of view a priority, for what you've written to get the result you want.

Written communication makes thoughts 'real'. As a writer I've had great ideas, but when I attempt to write them down, they suddenly become ordinary. When you write, you are trying to transform something that is alive inside of your brain, into something that is alive in the brain of your reader, through the sole medium of the printed word.

Written communication fixes responsibility

Writing things down clarifies your goals to others and assigns responsibility.

When your words are in black and white, you're putting

your thoughts out there for others to see. While you should think like the reader when writing something, remember that responsibility for what you've written is always yours as the author.

Don't qualify. Often people will write a statement that isn't a statement. They'll qualify it, which makes the meaning unclear.

For example:

In my opinion . . .

Of course it's your opinion if you're writing it.

It appears that . . .

It either is or isn't. Of course it's filtered through your perception, so it appears that way to you.

Qualifiers are the written way of trying to distance yourself from what you're writing. You may be doing this subconsciously. But, remember, responsibility is critical to being a leader and to being successful.

When writing, be careful of subconscious negatives. These tend to go hand-in-hand with using unnecessary words and phrases. Too often people put words, phrases and sentences in their writing that actually negate what they are trying to achieve with their communication.

For example, after finishing a manuscript, aspiring novelists have to write query letters, which is the equivalent of a resume for the book and writer. These are sent to agents and editors, as authors begin the long road toward trying to get published. When I teach, I spend a lot of time on the cover letter, pointing out common mistakes. One is subconscious negatives. Words or sentences that reflect negatively on the writer or the book. Starting a query letter with the phrase, "I hope you like the book," for example, is a subconscious negative. It indicates fear and uncertainty, because you're telling the person you don't have confidence in what you've done.

Often, query letters bad-mouth the very business the writers is trying to get into, by making comments about how difficult it is to get published and the lack of acumen on agents and editors' parts to see the author's brilliance.

Take the Challenge: Exercise 32

You have been doing written communications exercises through this book. Getting thoughts out of your head and into the real world. Look back on the exercises you've done so far and see how many times you qualified your answers or put subconscious negatives in your writing. Find two and rewrite them, removing the qualifiers.

Standing Operating Procedures Codify and Help Change Habits

Standing Operating Procedures (SOPs) are anything written down that delineates how things should be done. They can serve many purposes, which we will cover shortly. The key part of the first sentence of this paragraph is *written down*.

Once more: Writing something down makes it real. It also makes it easily available. It reduces confusion and misunderstanding.

Every job I've ever done, I've ended up writing an SOP for it. Usually I do this because, surprisingly to me, no one before me did it, even when it was part of *their* job. I also did it so I could better understand what I was supposed to be doing.

When I finished my Special Forces training at Fort Bragg, I was issued orders assigning me to the 10th Special Forces Group (Airborne) at Ft Devens, MA. I was assigned as a team's executive officer. After being in-briefed by the team leader, he asked me if I had any questions. The first thing I did was ask him for the team's SOP, as I had been taught to do at Fort Bragg. I was surprised when he told me they didn't have one. He had several explanations why they didn't need one, but ultimately, in retrospect, the primary reason was no one had taken the initiative to write one, because writing an SOP is a very time consuming process. It's a 'front-end'-'back-end' deal. You put the work in on the front end to save you considerably more time in the long run on the back end. Unfortunately, too often, people are overwhelmed up front and don't see the larger and long range picture.

When I took command of my own A-Team a few months later, once again, the first thing I asked was where was the team SOP. I had been taught at Fort Bragg in the Qualification Course that every team should have an SOP. After my previous experience, I wasn't too surprised when I was told the team didn't have one written down. They 'knew' what they needed to do, I was told. Right. And even if *they* did, how was *I* supposed to 'know' it?

So we began writing the team SOP. Basically, I began formalizing what everyone said they 'knew'. I not only drew from my team members' expertise, I went to other teams and found those who did have SOPs and got copies. I went to the company headquarters and talked to the Sergeant Major who had extensive combat experience and got him to help, giving us some tips—seemingly small, but ones that could save your life in combat.

The team SOP when completed was rather detailed and a living document that we constantly refined as we tested concept in it and learned what worked and what didn't. The beginning of it was mine and my team sergeant's policy letters, spelling out our philosophy for leading the team.

My team sergeant was direct and to the point. Here were some of his choicer lines:

Nothing is impossible to the man who doesn't have to do it.

Smith & Wesson beats four aces.

The latest information hasn't been put out yet.

There are two types of soldiers– the steely eyed killer and the beady eyed minion.

Here are some excerpts from mine:

Most basic tenet of teamwork is honesty.

With rank & privilege comes responsibility.

Everyone is a leader.

We do everything together.

If you have a problem with someone with higher rank, let me know.

Keep a positive attitude.

Discipline stays at team level.

Be on time.

Keep your sense of humor. You'll need it.

After the policy letters, we then specified who on the team was responsible for what. We took much of this from the field manual for Special Forces that had this information. Again, as mentioned earlier, you can help yourself tremendously when writing an SOP to check out what is already out there. Someone, somewhere, probably wrote one just like what you want to write. Also, your SOP, like your goals, should be in alignment, with higher level SOPs.

We then covered numerous tactical situations and codified how each team member would act. Then we would train on those SOPs until the actions became instinctual.

SOPs Codify and Set Standards

When I was first published I attended a continuing education class on magazine writing. I didn't have plans to write articles, but I figured it was a form of writing so I would learn something. I was trying to get out of my tunnel vision. The instructor gave out a thin comb-bound booklet covering the material he was going to teach. I thought this was a good idea and when I was getting ready to teach my first writing class, I did the same.

My first draft of what I called my *Fiction Writer's Toolkit: A Guide To Writing Novels and Getting Published* was eleven pages long. That's how much I *consciously* knew about the subject matter, even though I'd already had three books published. As the years progressed and I wrote more books and taught more, I would continuously update the *Toolkit*. After eight years it became over ninety-thousand words long and was eventually published by Writer's Digest as *The Novel Writer's Toolkit: A Guide To Writing Great Fiction and Getting It Published*. Does that mean I learned so much new stuff over the years? Yes, but what I also did was begin to move things I 'knew' from my subconscious to my conscious. There was no way I would have published three books if all I knew was eleven pages worth of material about writing books. An SOP is an excellent way to formalize things you already 'know', but aren't quite sure that you know.

This book you are reading began in the same way, as I began to write down what we had done in Special Forces, to codify it in a usable format.

Special Operations has always relied on SOPs. Back in the lineage section I mentioned Roger's Rangers. If you get a copy of the current US Army Ranger Handbook, which every good Infantry and Special Forces officer should be packing, in the very beginning are a list of Roger's Rules of Rangering. The first Rangers were formed in 1756 and Rogers wrote his rules in 1759 after three years of combat experience on the frontier. Some of these sound quite simple but they were learned, as many of the lessons in this book were, at the cost of blood:

Don't forget nothing.

Tell the truth about what you see and do.

When you're on the march, act the way you would if you were sneaking up on a deer. See the enemy first.

Don't never take a chance you don't have to.

When we camp, half the party stays awake while the other half sleeps.

Don't ever march home the same way. Take a different route so you won't be ambushed.

And so on—all very basic, but rules that are constantly violated every day by military forces. At the cost of blood.

Whatever your job is, you should have an SOP for it. And it should be written so that someone with no background can achieve a base level of functioning in the job for a short period of time. Other SOPs should lay out the way your organization works. The way things really work, not how you want someone to think they work.

One issue our A-Teams had was putting together Off

Post Training Packets. These were requests to conduct training off the military reservation, which was the norm as the facilities were limited. It was almost a magical event when a team put one together, mixing and matching various forms that they had to get the support needed for this. When I was the operations officer, I went over to the Support Battalion and asked them what they really needed. They had a single form that covered everything. I asked what they did with all the extra forms that teams took a lot of time to figure out? They tossed them in the trash. But no one at Support had ever bothered to send a message the other way to inform the teams of the time and effort they were wasting. I put together a packet for every team with what they really needed and told them they could toss all the extra stuff they were wasting time on.

SOPs are a great way to codify habits you want to develop and also list habits you want to avoid. Writing them down and posting them some place you can consistently see them helps keep you in the real world. As you can tell by having gotten this far in the book, you won't be able to keep all you've learned or need to do in your head. That's why the exercises require you to write things down. To make them more 'real' than simply thinking about them.

Failure to follow SOPs lays the groundwork for disaster, as is failing to study history. You will see this shortly in the Blood Lesson of The Woman Who Was.

SOPs should be followed, but also evaluated in the face of changing circumstances. SOPs are not written in stone. SOPs need to be checked every once in a while to make sure that they are applicable and that they are being followed. Having a nice looking binder with wonderfully written SOPs does you no good if you don't read them or follow them. And SOPs that are out of date can cause more harm than good. They should be constantly updated based on After Action Reviews, which we will cover shortly.

An example of a Standing Operating Procedure I use is a list of my Blind Spots. Those things I have a tendency to do that have a negative effect. I use that list to remind me of character flaws I'm trying to overcome. This list often stops me from screwing up. Another SOP I use is for my physical fitness routine. I list out what I'm doing on each day of the week (bike, run, kayak on certain days) so I have a consistent program. Many of the exercises you've done in this book have given you answers that you can post and use as personal SOPs.

Take the Challenge: Exercise 33

Pick an aspect of your life (job, hobby, physical fitness program, etc) and begin to write the SOP for it. Start with the goal (What) you laid out for this way back in Tool One, in exercise 4.

Oral Communication:

Oral communication is faster than written. And in the speed

of your response lies the danger. Many times, oral communication is action taken in response to something.

You must be careful whenever you react. You must be careful not to speak—to act—without thinking.

Many of the things we discussed under written communication apply to oral communication. Oral communication, however, is more situational. A large part of it depends on whom you are speaking to. A successful person considers his audience's point of view and directs the conversation accordingly, without losing his own point of view.

For example, during the first day of West Point Beast Barracks, called R-Day, for Reception Day, new cadets are run through a meat-grinder of checkpoints and instant discipline. A checklist is pinned to the new cadet's uniform with all the places they have to visit that day for in-processing. They are instructed to report to the 'Man in the red sash,' an upperclassmen who checks the list and direct cadets onward. Of course, it isn't that easy.

When you first report to the man in the red sash, you are carrying your bags from home. The man orders you to "*Drop the bags.*" Most cadets, being normal people, will lower the bags to the ground. The man then orders them to pick the bags back up, and then once more orders them to "*Drop the bags,*" his voice going up an octave. This process continues, until the bewildered new cadets realize they are supposed to drop the bags instantly upon receiving the order. It is the beginning of teaching cadets to instantly and literally obey orders without question.

Since you're not in Beast Barracks, don't be afraid to ask questions or express uncertainty, when listening to others speak. If others aren't getting their message across to you, the misunderstanding is not necessarily your fault. Lord Cardigan should have taken a second or two to ask the

156156156156156 BOB MAYER

courier exactly what the objective was, rather than accepting a vague gesture from the courier.

This is particularly crucial in phone conversations, where you aren't given many non-verbal cues. The phone is a necessary tool of our society and one over which much business and personal communication is conducted. For your business, it pays to keep a log of all phone conversations, just like you keep a log of all written messages that come through the mail or via the Internet. In oral communication, ask and answer as many questions as are necessary, to make sure you and the person you're speaking with are on the same page—BEFORE action is taken.

When communicating through the spoken word, evaluate who you are talking to, and adjust accordingly. We've covered differing points of view several times already. In addition to that, you need to gauge the intellectual and experience level of the people you're speaking with, to ensure that they can understand what you're saying.

Dialogue, the actual words that are said, reveal a great deal about people. If you listen and observe carefully you can often uncover true motivation. Conflict and disagreement can escalate quickly, because a few seemingly innocent words are used.

Be careful when you use slang or abbreviations. Slang often reflects negatively on the speaker. If you use abbreviations, make sure people know what they mean. Too often people assume that the other person understands them, and sometimes the other person isn't willing to admit their ignorance. Using abbreviations can also give the hearer the impression that you're trying to distance yourself from, or intellectually elevate yourself above them. It pays to be slow and patient and explain things as you need to.

It pays to be slow and patient and explain things. I'm

going to discuss the operations order shortly, but I want to talk about an incident that occurred when I was briefing an order that included not only supporting troops from the 82nd Airborne, but indigenous forces, as was par for many Special Forces missions.

I took my time and slowly went through the order, making sure I explained everything in detail *and* making sure everyone I was talking to, including the foreign troops, clearly understood the order.

A captain from the 82nd Airborne told me afterward that the long, detailed operations order I'd just given wouldn't cut it in the 82nd. I wanted to reply—but didn't, sticking with my golden rule—that I was never going to be in the 82nd Airborne so I didn't care. And that there was no time pressure under the scenario we were working, so the time issue shouldn't have a problem. The interesting thing was that every foreign officer came up to me afterwards and said that was the first OPORDER that they had understood completely.

Too often people get caught up in format, not content. A format is nothing more than a tool to follow. Use it if it works. But if it doesn't work, improvise.

The successful person makes sure the content of what they are trying to communicate gets across regardless of format.

Communicate: The Artist's Imagination

As a teacher I've worked with thousands of aspiring writers. As I've said, the percentage who actually were open to learning and improving their craft was around the infamous 5% mark. The key to success for those few was that they got out of their own point of view and considered the reader.

They understood that writing a novel is about entertaining and informing the reader, not about the author's own validation.

To be a successful communicator, you have to make what you're saying is about the people receiving the communication, not about you—the person sending it.

TOOL EIGHT: TAKE
COMMAND OF YOUR CHANGE

A successful person must:

- Be able to lead themselves
- Be able to interact with others and lead them.

You can't count on others to bring you to a successful level in life.

Others can help. But the only person you can count on one hundred percent of the time is yourself. Because of this, you must develop and master personal leadership.

To be different from the majority, to be successful, you must find your way out of the pack and along a difficult road. If you don't exercise personal leadership, you will be under the control of those around you, whose goals might not be in line with your own goals.

No one else can hand you what you want to achieve—you have to earn it.

The Green Beret Guide

**Special Forces Assessment
and Selection Thought:**
*Challenges can be stepping stones
or stumbling blocks.
It's all in your perspective.*

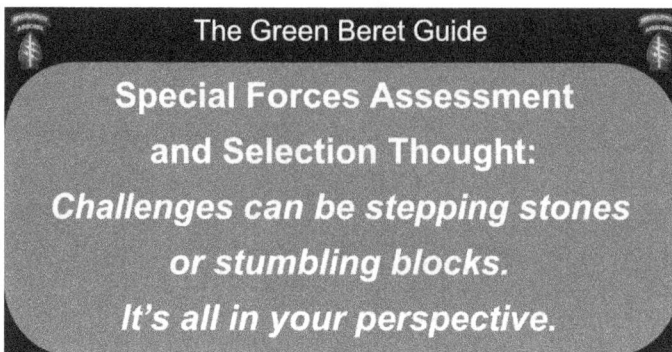

Blood Lesson: The Woman Who Was

We've examined the story of the Man Who Never Was--an example of goal-setting and one-sentence problem solving. This Blood Lesson is about a very brave woman who, most tragically, did exist.

One of the first covert female radio operator sent into occupied France was Noor Inayat Khan. While she displayed extraordinary bravery and paid the ultimate price, she failed to exercise the personal leadership required to assess her situation—a failure that cost others their lives as well.

The Problem

As World War II raged on, a resistance movement began to flourish in the occupied countries. To assist these movements, the British Special Operations Executive (SOE) parachuted in units called Jedburgh Teams to assist the Resistance (these were the forerunners of Special Forces). In the fog of war, spy-versus-spy betrayal was a constant factor. Despite having the best intentions, an operative needed to exercise personal leadership to evaluate every situation and prevent disaster.

Khan came from an Indian Muslim family. Her elder brother eventually became the head of the Sufi Order International. She was living with her family in Paris when the Germans invaded. They fled to England. Khan joined the Women's Auxiliary Air Force and was trained as a wireless (radio) operator. Because of her fluency in French and her wireless skills, she was recruited by the SOE as an operative.

Some of her trainers felt she was an unsuitable candidate for covert work, because her ethnic background and beauty caused her to stand out in a crowd. Nevertheless on the night of 16 June 1943 she was flown into France and joined a Resistance network.

Within a month and a half the network was rolled up by the Gestapo. There is some speculation that the British knew the network had already been compromised and sent Khan in, expecting her to be captured and give up 'information' she had been fed in training—false information. A living version of the *Man Who Never Was*. Some say she was betrayed by another female agent out of jealousy because Khan had become the lover of that woman's ex.

The Solution

Although Khan was brave and did not speak under interrogation, she'd been overly-conscientious in her job and had violated Standing Operating Procedures—she'd kept copies of all her messages. The Germans, therefore, were able to begin transmitting, imitating her.

Her handlers in London allegedly failed to note anomalies in 'her' transmissions. They dropped three more agents into France because of one of these transmissions—the Gestapo arrested the agents on the drop zone. Again, there is speculation the handlers knew exactly what they were doing—executing a version of *The Man Who Never Was*, except with live bodies this time.

Khan—and one of the agents captured because of her messages—were taken to Dachau and executed on 13 September 1944.

The Lesson

As you learned under *Character*, any trait taken to an extreme is dangerous. Khan took her passion for her duty to an extreme that back-fired. Certainly, her courage cannot be questioned. But her command of herself and the situation wasn't solid.

She'd not followed SOPs and this mistake cost others their lives.

Noor Inayat Khan was posthumously awarded a George Cross, Britain's highest award for gallantry not on the battle-field. The citation reads:

The KING has been graciously pleased to approve the post-humous award of the GEORGE CROSS to:—Assistant Section Officer Nora INAYAT-KHAN (9901), Women's Auxiliary Air Force. Assistant Section Officer Nora INAYAT-KHAN was the first woman operator to be infiltrated into enemy occupied France, and was landed by Lysander aircraft on 16th June, 1943. During the weeks immediately following her arrival, the Gestapo made mass arrests in the Paris Resistance groups to which she had been detailed. She refused however to abandon what had become the principal and most dangerous post in France, although given the opportunity to return to England, because she did not wish to leave her French comrades without communications and she hoped also to rebuild her group. She remained at her post therefore and did the excellent work which earned her a posthumous Mention in Despatches.

The Gestapo had a full description of her, but knew only her code name "Madeleine". They deployed considerable forces in their effort to catch her and so break the last remaining link with London. After 3 months she was betrayed to the Gestapo and taken to their H.Q. in the Avenue Foch. The Gestapo had found her codes and messages and were now in a position to work back to London. They asked her to co-operate, but she refused and gave them no information of any kind. She was imprisoned in one of the cells on the 5th floor of the Gestapo H.Q. and remained there for several weeks during which time she made two unsuccessful attempts at escape. She was asked to sign a declaration that she would make no further attempts but she refused and the Chief of the Gestapo obtained permission from Berlin to send her to Germany for "safe custody". She was the first agent to be sent to Germany.

Assistant Section Officer INAYAT-KHAN was sent to Karlsruhe in November; 1943, and then to Pforsheim where her cell was apart from the main prison. She was considered to be a particularly dangerous and unco-operative prisoner. The Director of the prison has also been interrogated and has confirmed that Assistant Section Officer INAYAT-KHAN, when interrogated by the Karlsruhe Gestapo, refused to give any information whatsoever, either as to her work or her colleagues.

She was taken with three others to Dachau Camp on the 12th September, 1944. On arrival, she was taken to the crematorium and shot.

Assistant Section Officer Inayat-Khan displayed the most conspicuous courage, both moral and physical over a period of more than 12 months.

The Purpose of Leadership

A leader is a person who makes decisions and then implements a course of action. Since a successful person is someone who takes action, that person is, by definition, a leader.

The first thing a leader must do is set goals. Then the leader must make a decision, leading to a course of action that implements sustained change. Ultimately, a leader must take care of himself or herself, and then those around them.

The first person you must understand how to lead is yourself. That's why I spend so much time in *Area Two: Who* on character. You need to figure out your personality type and your blind spot. Successful people overcome their weaknesses, and the first step in doing that is identifying the weaknesses. This skill immediately separates those who want to be successful from the majority of the bell curve.

When I teach leadership, I focus first on getting leaders to look at themselves and their personal leadership before looking at their leadership of others. If you read Appendix I, you'll see an array of military leadership.

Special Operations Leadership

I believe the type of leadership we utilize in Special Operations is ideally suited to develop successful individual leadership. Units in Special Operations are small and the soldiers well trained and internally motivated. Their missions are usually above the military norm. Special Forces often operates far removed from the normal military chain of command.

There are two key elements of Special Operations leadership:

- Honesty
- Integrity

Honesty

Honesty is the foundation of respect. Without honesty, all other aspects of what you learn in this guide fall apart. Special Operations Forces, which conduct covert and secret operations, actually rely on honesty a great deal. You may find that curious. But it is the very nature of their missions that requires a higher degree of internal honesty from SOF members and teams.

Honesty is your key to dealing with those around you. You cannot expect people to be honest with you, if you aren't with them. And first and foremost, you need to be honest with yourself.

We all have secrets, and those secrets are often rooted in our deepest fears. Bringing your secrets into the light of day seems daunting. But in reality, once you've achieved this step, the result is rarely ever as bad as you expected it to be. Most people care more about themselves more than they do about you. Many people over-estimate how others are going to react to their secrets.

Take the Challenge: Exercise 34

Write down a truth about yourself that you've never told anyone.
Now write down why you haven't told anyone. What are you afraid would happen if you did? How does that fear hold you back?

Your honesty is the touchstone of good communication with those you interact with and those you lead. Remember, we teach people how to treat us.

I spoke with another Special Forces team leader about serving in Afghanistan. He made the point that the Afghanis treated American units differently, depending on how the American units first treated the Afghanis. Those teams that made themselves the honest, but bad-ass, sheriff in town were treated with respect.

Quickly admitting you are wrong—when you are—is a very powerful tool. It disarms those around you. It allows you to focus on fixing a problem rather than defending your position, which is already a bad one, since you're wrong. Admitting when you're wrong builds trust and allows for better communication—especially when you need help.

Take the Challenge: Exercise 35

Write down something you've done wrong in the past week.

Did you acknowledge the mistake to yourself? To anyone else?

Acknowledge it to someone else (especially the person you did the wrong to) and see what their reaction is?

When you are honest with other people, the threat of the unknown is reduced. The unknown is one of the great causes of fear. If people feel information is being withheld from them, they won't just ignore the feeling: they will start coming up with their own answers. Most of the time their imagination comes will come up with something far worse than the reality. Being honest induces trust and reduces fear, both within yourself and with others.

Integrity

The word integrity comes from the Latin word *integritas*, which means wholeness, completeness and entirety.

A Roman soldier, when being inspected by his Centurion, would strike his fist on the armor over his heart and shout "*Integritas.*" The armor was thicker there than anywhere else. In the same manner, your armor must be strongest around the most vulnerable parts of your successful character. Focusing on and building integrity is the best way to make sure that happens.

Integrity is the opposite of the emotional defenses around our defects. Integrity is the emotional shield around the part of us that is daring and willing to take risks.

People without integrity ignore their blind spots. And they hide other aspects of their character—often from themselves—because they are afraid. You must strive for completeness of character.

Completeness means all parts of your character are oriented toward the same goal rather than conflicting with one another. As you've learned, most people are the causes of their own failure. Accordingly, you can also be the cause of your success.

Integrity is outward-oriented, and requires that you understand the environment in which you live, and respect and understand those with whom you interact. It requires you to make your place in the world, and to make that place count—for your own good as well as others.

Command of self is taking action in the face of fear. Facing and dealing with fear is at the core of your ability to move from being ordinary to successful. How you deal with fear is also about how you apply honesty and integrity in your life, your actions and your decision making. Understanding your character and others is certainly important. And setting goals gives you direction.

The Circle of Success tools won't change anything by themselves, though. Not until your personal command begins to break you from the chains of fear.

Command of Self: The Artist's Imagination:

As an author it took me a long time to accept the reality of publishing: I control the quality of the books I write. I don't control the actions of my editor, my publisher, the book-store, etc. Trying to control those things is a waste of time and energy, and very emotionally draining. I learned to put that energy into the things I did control: my writing. To take command of that.

For a long time, I expected my agent to come up with a career plan for me. It took me years before I realized that my agents could never have done this. Each of them helped me, but I had to take command of, exercise personal leadership over, my career. I had to make the plan then ask them to help me implement it. I had to set the goals. And I had to take responsibility.

TOOL NINE: COMPLETE THE CIRCLE OF SUCCESS AND CHANGE

I ntroduction
        You've reached the last Tool. Is it clearer now why I call the nine tools of the Green Beret Guide the Circle of Success? Each of the Special Forces tools you've learned can be used alone. But true success comes when you integrate all the tools. You will continue to refine the exercises in this book as you go forward into your life.

That's why I positioned Command at Tool 8—because it is when you exercise personal leadership that you begin to pull all the tools together.

It is now time to Complete the Circle of Success.

The Green Beret Guide

Special Forces Assessment and Selection Thought:
You don't get to be number one by aspiring to be number two.

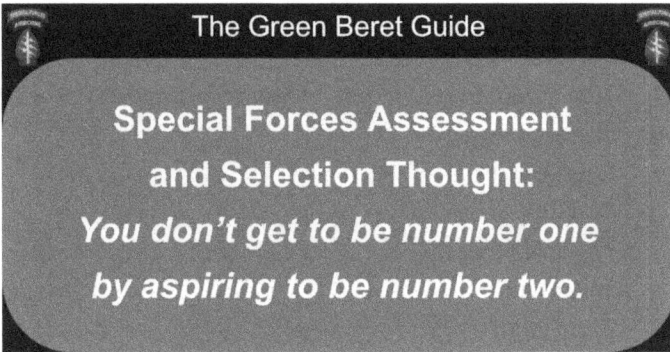

Blood Lesson: The Green Beret Guide

Every tool in this book is used to train Green Berets in the Special Forces Qualification Course (Q-Course).

The Problem

Special Forces was founded in 1952 by veterans of the Office of Strategic Service, like Colonel Volckman. These officers designed the course using the Blood Lessons they'd experienced in World War II.

The core concept of Special Forces has remained the same for over half a century, even as warfare and technology have evolved, and the threats facing our country have changed. The Q-Course has had to evolve, of course, and I was part of a committee that met at Fort Bragg in the mid-80s to modernize the Q-Course.

The Lesson

An applicant who passes Special Forces Assessment and Selection receives orders to permanently change their duty station to Fort Bragg. Only then do they face the Special Forces Qualification Course.

While evaluating Q-Course students, instructors focus on twelve attributes:

1. Intelligence.
2. Stability.
3. Physical fitness.
4. Judgment.
5. Motivation.
6. Decisiveness.
7. Accountability.
8. Influence.
9. Trustworthiness.
10. Team-work,
11. Maturity.
12. Communication.

Do these look familiar?

The Q-Course pulls together all the elements of the Green Beret Guide:

What

The course goal is to train Green Berets.

Why

The intent is to produce the best unconventional warrior on the planet.

Where

Training takes places in several locations, each designed to fit a particular expertise required to be a successful warrior.

Character

Assessment & Selection begins with instructors' character analysis of each student. Every step of Q-Course continues the ongoing evaluation.

Courage

Training is difficult, with a seventy-percent failure rate. Candidates must dig deep within themselves in order to pass.

Change

Successful candidates graduate the Q-Course as very different people than the ones who entered.

Command

Every graduate is taught to be a leader. Each will become part of an A-Team, where individual and group leadership is essential.

Communicate

They will be members of a successful team, and their primary mission will be to teach others. Without successful communication skills, they would fail, so communication is emphasized throughout Q-Course training.

Complete

The final Q-Course exercise is the most challenging— Robin Sage. All the skills a candidate has learned must be integrated and used at a successful level to succeed.

The Solution

On average, only thirty percent of students make it to the point of successfully completing Robin Sage. That's only thirty percent of the best of the best in the military.

Finally the student is no longer a student. Technically, at least. They ship out to various Special Forces field groups and are assigned to A-Teams. Where they quickly find out they have a lot to learn. Thus, the practical experience of operating on a real A-Team begins. So, just like you, they continue on their Circle of Success journey, constantly learning and improving for the rest of their lives.

The Lesson

The Q-Course continues to evolve and change, as more Blood Lessons are learned on battlefields all over the world. And you need to continue to evolve and change as you work your this program—as you rework and refine the Circle again and again on your own battlefields of life. What you have as you complete this book is a framework for a plan of action for change. A beginning. Never stop learning.

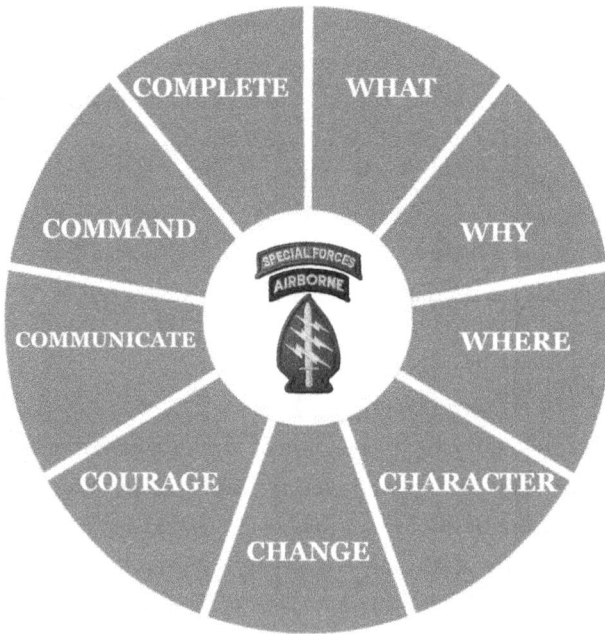

The Circle Of Success

Envision yourself standing at the center of the circle. All the tools converge at the center—you. They're all connected.

You've worked with all of them and have completed many exercises.

The Circle is not a one-time thing. Each pass from Tool Nine back to Tool One peels away another layer, circling closer and closer to uncovering the 'true' you that you desire to be.

Now it's time to come up with one more plan.

Take the Challenge: Exercise 36

Pick a new goal from your list in WINS: Exercise 1. One you've yet to work with. Perhaps one that has changed, that you've refined, as you've worked through the later tools and areas.

Take the rest of the tools in order, and write a short summary of what needs to happen under each tool, just like I did in the Blood Lesson for the Q-Course.

This is your chance to pull together everything you've learned about how to become successful in your life.

Review each tool as needed.

After Action Reviews

Once you've implemented your plan, it's time to use another Special Forces tool—the After Action Review (AAR). This is used by Special Forces to objectively determine if a mission's goal has been achieved. In fact, whenever you think you have finished doing something significant, you should conduct an AAR.

A person that won't look closely at themselves, is someone who is doomed to keep doing the same things wrong again and again.

Because simulated combat exercises are so difficult to observe and judge, the military designed the AAR to help the participants figure out what happened. It was only in the late 90s that the business world began picking up the concept, most likely a result of Army officers filtering into the civilian world and bringing what they had learned with them. A Harvard Business School professor wrote an article about it in the Harvard Business Review in 1993, which I suppose made it more high-brow than a squad of grunts sitting around trying to figure out what just happened. The most critical aspect of having an effective AAR is honesty. The first, and most important, question to be answered is, *"was the goal or mission accomplished?"* Given that your goal or mission was originally stated clearly in one sentence, the answer should be clear.

I have read several business books where it is said an AAR should not judge success or failure. I disagree with that. Why not? The theory is that focusing on success or failure will cause emotional conflict—if that's the case, then so be it. We succeed. We fail. We learn, adjust and move on. Successful people have to break through the conflict that comes with not succeeding all the time.

Remember the stages of change: denial, anger, bargaining, depression, acceptance. If failure at a goal is a conflict for you, it's one of your blind spots. Work through these changes until you've conquered the associated fear.

If the answer is yes, you achieved your goal, then pat yourself on the back, then see what fine-tuning needs to be done. If the answer is no, hunker down until the smoke clears—until you have solid answers from your AAR and know what changes need to be made to your plan.

Steps for an effective AAR:

1. Did you achieve your goal?
2. Review your plan. Did you follow your plan? If not, note the exceptions and variations you made. Did the rule breaking of the plan work? If it didn't, take responsibility.
3. Review the preparation for the activity—which means once more go through all the tools listed in this book, and now that the plan has been executed, determine if each tool was effectively applied to your plan. If not, note areas of improvement or refinement you could have made.
4. Summarize the events as they occurred, using a detailed timeline, with no commentary. Just the facts. Build a complete timeline of action.
5. Focus on why each specific action was taken. Whether each step of the plan was followed, or deviated from (which is not necessarily a bad thing).
6. Give particular focus to when fear played a role in your actions—this is the most difficult part of the AAR, but the most critical—fear is most

likely where your actions diverged from your plan.

7. Examine what role SOPs played. Did they work? Do they need to be revised?

8. Summarize areas of plan improvement and refinement, as well as alternative actions you could have taken to achieve a more successful result.

Take the Challenge: Exercise 37

Conduct an After-Action Review for your plan from Exercise 36. With your AAR done, incorporate all you've learned into a modified plan, then do it over again. Repeat as necessary until it achieves the change and goal you desire.

Rule Breaking

A successful person must have a sense of confidence that enables him to break the rules when needed. But he must also have a clearly-defined reason for breaking a rule.

There are three *rules* for rule breaking

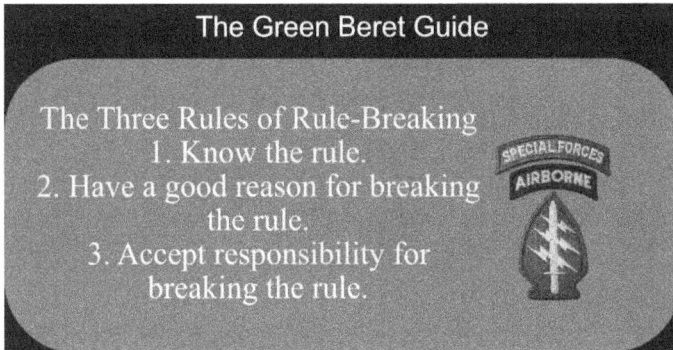

The Green Beret Guide

The Three Rules of Rule-Breaking
1. Know the rule.
2. Have a good reason for breaking the rule.
3. Accept responsibility for breaking the rule.

<u>Know the rule.</u>

Breaking a rule because you're ignorant of it is simply being, well, ignorant.

<u>Have good reason for breaking the rule.</u>

You know the rule. Objectively study how it factors into achieving plan success, and only break it if you think doing so will bring you greater success.

<u>Take responsibility for breaking the rule.</u>

If breaking the rule works out, great. If it doesn't, it's on you. Own the result, either way. That's integrity—a cornerstone of a successful person's character.

To succeed in life and break out of the ordinary, you are going to have to break some rules.

Complete: The Artist's Imagination

The components of a successful novel can be broken down into Circle of Success tools:

- WHAT: the idea and plot
- WHY: Intent
- WHERE: Setting

- CHARACTER: in the story is key and understand yours as a writer
- CHANGE: Character arc and learning to be a better writer
- COURAGE: you have to dare to be different
- COMMUNICATE: the writing itself
- COMMAND: as the author, you are responsible for the book
- COMPLETE: you have to finish the book

Like the tools you've learned in this guide, each story component by itself does not make a novel. A writer must pull all the aspects of his story together into one coherent whole, before the reader will follow him and his characters on the journey (the mission) he's created.

For most writers, trying to define the entirety of a novel before doing the first bit of planning is an overwhelming task. It's often much more effective and less intimidating for the writer to develop a story piece by piece, building the whole out of the parts.

The Green Beret Guide is your opportunity to focus on piece-by-piece development, as you build toward your successful whole. Work on each tool, one at a time. And gradually, you will learn how to put the pieces together and win.

It takes continuous work on every tool, and a lifetime commitment to continue following the Circle of Success—pulling each tool closer to the next until they intertwine—to create an integrated, successful person.

Area Three Conclusion: DARES, the Green Beret Guide

.   .   .

You've learned everything you need to know about the Circle of Success. You have the tools you need to Conquer Fear and Succeed.

Now the choice lies with you. You must determine the path your life takes.

One Final Blood Lesson: Robin Sage

The culminating exercise of the Special Forces Qualification Course is Robin Sage. Robin Sage is designed to be as realistic a mission simulation as can be accomplished in a training environment.

The Problem

Robin Sage is the fourth phase of the Q-Course. It lasts a total of thirty-eight days. Students are transported to Camp Mackall. The students are broken down into A-Teams and required to put their successful knowledge and skills to use in a nineteen-day problem-solving Field Training Exercise (and yes, this is a Blood Lesson as men have died during this 'exercise'.)

Robin Sage is an unconventional warfare exercise, in which students must not only deal with other students, but also counterinsurgent and guerrilla personnel, auxiliary personnel, and instructors. Realism is stressed above all else.

The student teams must train a mock guerilla force in a hostile environment, using civilians in the surrounding community as their auxiliary manpower. This exercise ranges over approximately fifty thousand square miles of North Carolina country-side. By the conclusion of Robin

Sage, the students have been placed in many stressful situations where they are required to use their individual skills,
leadership skills, and their abilities to work in adverse and
ambiguous conditions.

One thing to remember about the lengths of these
various courses and exercises: don't think of each 'day' in
civilian terms of an eight to ten hour workday, and then
home for a beer. The 19 days for Robin Sage is a grueling,
often spirit-breaking, 24/7 experience.

Solution

The evaluation of a Special Forces student in Robin Sage
is about much more than completing his mission. It's
about being the best soldier he can be and operating on a
team. Students are graded not only on how well they
accomplish their individual tasks, but also how well their
team does.

They are graded on all aspects of this guide, not just a
particular specialty.

Thinking outside of the problem is important. Most of
the scenarios in Robin Sage are set up as lose-lose. There is
no good or right solution. Students must think quickly and
come up with the best possible solution under extreme
stress, just like they will on deployment.

Do you remember in the *Star Trek* movie (*Wrath of Khan*)
when Captain Kirk talks about being at Star Fleet Academy
and being the only officer to have passed the *Kobayashi
Maru* simulator program? (And redone in the Star Trek
prequel). The basic problem and the opening of the movie
was set up this way: A Star Fleet ship which the student
commands is patrolling near the neutral zone. A distress
call is received from a disabled Federation vessel inside the

neutral zone. An enemy warship is approaching from the other side. A vessel more powerful than the one the student commands. The choices seem obvious: ignore the distress call (which violates the law of space) or go to its aid (violating the neutral zone) and face almost certain destruction from the enemy vessel. As you can see, both choices are bad.

What Kirk did was sneak into the computer center the night before he was scheduled to go through the simulation and change the parameters so that he could successfully save the vessel without getting destroyed. Would you have thought of that? Was it cheating? If you ain't cheating you ain't trying. It's not cheating when it succeeds. Was anyone hurt by this? No.

Successfully thinking outside the parameters is a sign of the elite.

You might consider your life to be Robin Sage, a constant testing environment where you can get better and more confident with each new experience.

Knowledge is Useless, If Not Used

If you've read this book up to this point, it was most likely the equivalent of trying to take a sip of water from a fire hydrant. A lot came at you. Some of it seemed very simple and basic to you, and some of it you probably still don't 'get' yet. Even some of the simple stuff may have appeared easy, but once you tried doing it, you found just how deceiving appearances can be.

Do you want to be successful?

I asked this question at the beginning of the book. Now that you are at the end, you have a better idea of what taking a successful life path will require—what it will mean to succeed in the face of fear.

Now, you need to ask yourself the same question—and you need to answer it again honestly. A half-effort won't get you where you want to be. A ninety-five percent effort will not succeed. You must be totally committed to the choice you've made—to the Circle of Success.

Take the Challenge: Exercise 38
Time to pull it all together. Fold a piece of paper in thirds. Label the left column MOE. In it, write down the answers to these questions—make them real:
While 'drinking' from the hydrant that is this book:
What stood out?
What angered you?
What made you afraid?
What motivated you?
What excited you?
What did you think was dumb?
What did you think was smart?
What did you think wouldn't work?

What do you think was something you could use right away?
What did you want to know more about?

YOUR ANSWERS to these questions are new moments of enlightenment for you to analyze and build future decisions and actions from—using everything you've learned.

Take the Challenge: Exercise 39
Your decisions. In the center column of the paper from exercise 38, label it Decisions, and write down what decision you want to make regarding your moments of enlightenment.

Take the Challenge: Exercise 40

Your sustained action. In the right column of the paper from exercise 39, label it Sustained Actions, and write down what sustained action you will have to do in order to change.

As you've learned, the Circle of Success is an ongoing cycle of change—one moment of enlightenment leads to another, and then another. If reading and working through the Green Beret Guide tools has helped you rise out of the mundane and fear-filled—it's not time to kick back, light a cigar and think you've made it made.

To continue to improve you must work through the Circle again. All the Green Beret Guide challenges are listed once more in Appendix B. Do them again. All of them. And then do them again.

With each new pass, compare the new answers you write down, to the ones you've written previously. You should see your point of view changing each time. Your new reality, compared to your world before.

Integration and Tightness

The Green Beret Guide is made up of many pieces and parts. Three major areas, with three tools each, that make up the Circle of Success. Tightness of effort and integrity is a sign of the successful. I've made numerous cross-references throughout this book, indicating where one subject touched on another. Those cross-references show you the tightness your efforts need to achieve—how much one part of the circle depends on another.

As you saw in some of the Blood Lessons, succeeding in several areas of the Green Beret Guide, but not all, can lead to disaster. In fact, partial success can be a very dangerous thing. Anayat Khan certainly had tremendous Courage, but problems in Command and Communication cost lives.

It is essential to keep all the parts of the Green Beret Guide and your Circle of Success tightly integrated.

LIVING A SUCCESSFUL LIFE

Living a successful life—really succeeding—begins and ends with you. Many people fail and succumb to fear as they try to follow a successful path. They expend their energy trying to change the world around them, rather than themselves, and the world resists.

Dare to focus on becoming the person you want to be first. Focus on understanding your own true path. Once you achieve a measure of success in that, only then is it time to move out into the world, and dare to focus on how you interact with others and the path's they're living.

Good luck and all the best!

THE END

https://www.bobmayer.com/books-by-bob-mayer/

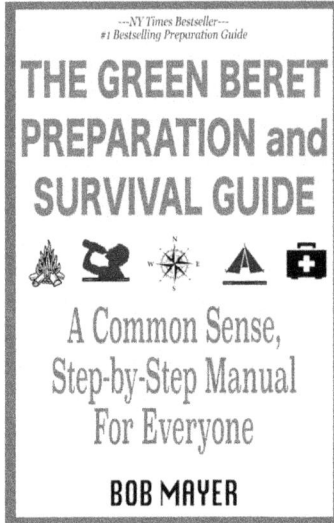

Note that there is now a workbook that walks you through doing an Area Study: *The Green Beret Area Study Workbook: How To Save Time and Money By Focusing Your Preparation*

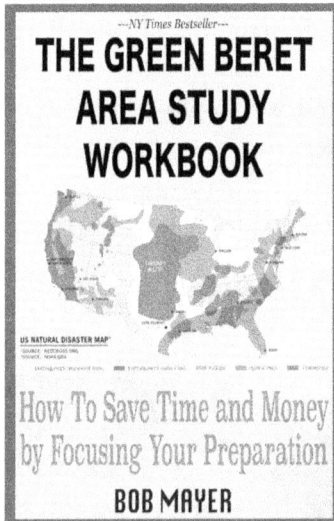

Author's Note: since things are constantly changing, please email if you find outdated links. Also, please send comments, suggestions, etc. to: bob@bobmayer.com

If you want a pocket-sized version of just the survival portion of this manual, it is titled: **The Green Beret Pocket-Sized Survival Guide**
https://www.bobmayer.com/books-by-bob-mayer/

I also have a series studying great disasters of the past in order to learn how to avoid similar ones in the future. They cover events ranging from Titanic to Challenger to the Housing Bubble.
The Green Beret Guide to Great Disasters: What Caused them and How We Can Prevent Future Ones

APPENDIX A: THE CIRCLE
OF SUCCESS PATH

1. WHAT do you want to change and achieve?

Write down each goal you want to achieve in one sentence.

Check the verb in each sentence: and make sure it is a positive and something you control.

Make sure the outcome of each goal is something that you can observe and know when you've achieved it.

Check your goals for inherent conflict.

2. WHY do you want to change and achieve your goals?

Using your one-sentence goals, write down WHY you want to achieve each goal: ie I am doing this goal for this reason.

Examine your WHY for options on how you can achieve the goal.

Examine your WHY to set boundaries for your goal, so you don't go to extremes.

3. WHERE will change occur?

Examine your environment and see who and what will aid you in achieving your WHAT and changing.

Figure out who and what are hindering you from achieving your WHAT and changing and take steps to get rid of those distractions or negate them.

Research your WHAT (goals) and WHY (intent).

4. Understand your CHARACTER.

Character is your core personality, both positive and negative.

Study your actions to determine your character and true nature.

Work on possessing the character traits of successful people:

Open-mindedness; willingness to surrender when wrong; balancing desire & contentment; having patience and self-discipline; using an active imagination and setting goals.

Understand that emotion is more powerful than intellect.

Figure out your Character, both strengths and weaknesses, by profiling your habits and also by comparing yourself to character templates, such as the Myers-Briggs.

5. What is CHANGE and how do you do it?

Understand and implement the three steps of change:

1. Have a moment of enlightenment.

2. Make a decision.

3. Implement sustained action.

6. How do you build the COURAGE to change?

Going back to character, look at the opposite character

type of yours in the Myers-Briggs and see what you are afraid of doing, then force yourself to do that.

Find your Blind Spot by using the traits, needs flaws diagram.

Expand your Comfort Zone by repeatedly venturing into your Courage Zone.

Catastrophe plan the various aspects of your life, predicting what the worst case scenario would be, and then being ready to face it.

7. COMMUNICATE your change to the world.

The purpose of communication is to evoke a desired response.

Writing things down make them real and delineates responsibility.

Read and listen carefully to get the true message being communicated by others.

8. Take COMMAND of your change.

You are in Command of everything you say and do.

You must have honesty and integrity at part of your personal leadership traits.

9. COMPLETE the Circle of Success and change.

Integrate and align the previous eight tools.

Use the three rules of rule-breaking to break out of the mundane and become successful:

1. Know the rule.

2. Have a good reason for breaking the rule.

3. Take responsibility for breaking the rule.

APPENDIX B: ALL CHALLENGES

Take the Challenge: Exercise 1

Write down the one thing you fear the most.

(The fear in your head is not in the real world. Writing down your fear externalizes it, so you can take action to conquer it in the real world).

Take the Challenge: Exercise 2

Write down the one thing that motivates you the most.

Take the Challenge: Exercise 3

In one sentence, write down a short-term goal that you want to achieve in the next seven days.

Take the Challenge: Exercise 4

Divide a piece of lined paper into four equal columns.

Label each column: What, Why, Where, Done.

Under the first column, WHAT, write a subordinate goal for each of the areas that are applicable to you in which you want to achieve a goal in the next week (nothing major, just a basic, simple goal).

Take the Challenge: Exercise 5

Using the four-column sheet from Exercise 4, fill out the second column. Next to each WHAT, list the WHY in the second column. I am doing X (what) for reason Y (why).

Take the Challenge: Exercise 6

Take a piece of paper. Fold it in thirds. In the left column write down the What you listed in column three of Exercise 4.

Label the middle column *My WHERE As It Is Now.*

Label the right column *My WHERE As It Should Be.*

List in the middle column those people and things that currently are part of your WHERE and how they effect it.

List in the right column how you would like your WHERE to be in order to be a positive environment.

Take the Challenge: Exercise 7

Using the four-column sheet from Exercise 4, fill out the third column. Next to each WHAT and WHY, list the WHERE in the third column.

Take the Challenge: Exercise 8

Using the four-column sheet from Exercise 4, fill out the third column. Next to each WHAT and WHY, list the WHERE in the third column.

Using your four column sheet from Exercise 4, pick one of the What's. Using the Why and Where you've already added, apply the CARVER formula to the goal to see if you can achieve it. If you can, then you can check column four—Done.

This doesn't mean the What is actually done; it means your planning for it is done. You can apply this formula to all your Whats.

Take the Challenge: Exercise 9
Define Yourself in one sentence.

Take the Challenge: Exercise 10
On the same sheet as Exercise 9, describe a moment when you were under extreme stress and pressure and had to make a decision. List the cause of the stress and pressure.

Take the Challenge: Exercise 11
On the same sheet as exercises 9 and 10, describe your reaction to that moment and the decision you made.

In retrospect, was it a good decision, or could you have chosen better?

Take the Challenge: Exercise 12
Describe the last time you were told you were doing something wrong and how you responded to it.

Describe your reaction in terms of the five parts of the Kubler-Ross scale.

Did you make it to acceptance and change?

If not, where did you stop and why?

Take the Challenge: Exercise 13
Take a piece of paper. Draw a line down the middle. Label the left side TO DO. Label the right side DONE.

List down the left side everything you have to do tomorrow.

Then, when you do one of your TO DO's, cross it off *and* write what you've done on the right side. Thus you can literally see your balance between desire and contentment on one page for one day.

Take the Challenge: Exercise 14

Look at your TO DO/DONE list from Exercise 13. Are there some TO DO's that aren't really needed? That you've actually had on your TO DO list a long time and never gotten around to? Maybe you shouldn't do them at all. Close some doors. Get rid of options that distract from your main goals.

Take the Challenge: Exercise 15

Remember the four column What, Why, Where, Done list you began in Exercise 4? For every What that has not been Done, pencil in a deadline for when it should be done.

The clock is now ticking.

Take the Challenge: Exercise 16

Describe the last time you felt anger or guilt? (If you can't remember, then try to focus on the *next* time you feel either of those emotions). Write the event down. What specifically provoked the emotion? Why did this situation touch your flash point? Simply understanding this dynamic will make you stronger the next time your flash point is touched.

Take the Challenge: Exercise 17

For the next 24 hours, write down everything you do.

Simply list every action, and how long it took, without comment. Let the list sit for several days. Then look at the list with an open mind. Describe what kind of person would do these things?

Then answer these questions: "Is this the kind of person I want to be? Are these the things I really want to be spending my time doing?"

Take the Challenge: Exercise 18

Pick A or B for each of the four areas that best describe you:

Take the Challenge: Exercise 19

Fold a piece of paper in thirds. On the left third, write down three Moments of Enlightenment you've had since beginning this book.

Take the Challenge: Exercise 20

Using the paper from exercise 19, in the middle column, write down a decision to change for each of the three Moments of Enlightenment.

Take the Challenge: Exercise 21

For each decision to change you listed in Exercise 20, in the right column, define the sustained action you would have to do to achieve the change you desire.

Take the Challenge: Exercise 22

Using your goal-aligned training program from Exercises 19-21, list the standards you need to achieve to sustain change. Post these standards where you can see them every day. Make the standards external goals that can clearly be assessed—you either achieve the standard, or you don't.

Take the Challenge: Exercise 23

In one word, record what you believe to be your greatest character trait. (the list above is only a suggested one)

Take the Challenge: Exercise 24

Using that trait, write down the corresponding need and potential flaw (blind spot).

Take the Challenge: Exercise 25

Describe the last time you wanted to do something you knew was the right thing to do, but you didn't do it. What kept you from doing it?

Take the Challenge: Exercise 26

Based on what you've uncovered in this Tool and under Character, list those traits, needs and flaws that you feel compromise your character. Then list the fears (blinds spots) that you suspect hurt you.

Take the Challenge: Exercise 27

Think back to the last really bad thing that happened to you. Write it down. Then write down the warning signs that were present before it happened, but that you didn't focus on.

These warning signs are fear indicators that you should write down and post so that you can see them every day. Read them, focus on them, and examine if they are coming up again with regard to something else in your life.

Take the Challenge: Exercise 28

Based on your answer to Exercise 26, pick one flaw and write down one positive act that would challenge you to face that blind spot, act in the face of fear and enter your courage zone?

Take the Challenge: Exercise 29

For the next week, do this one positive act every day. By the end of the week, your Comfort Zone will have increased.

Take the Challenge: Exercise 30

Fold a piece of paper in half, and on the left side, for the following areas, write down a potential catastrophe that could occur:

Physical:

Financial:

Natural disaster:

Work:

Relationship:

The next major task you have to do:

Take the Challenge: Exercise 31

On the right side of the paper from exercise 30, write out your plan in case the catastrophe occurs and then make the necessary preparations.

Take the Challenge: Exercise 32

You have been doing written communications exercises through this book. Getting thoughts out of your head and into the real world. Look back on the exercises you've done so far and see how many times you qualified your answers or put subconscious negatives in your writing.

Find two and rewrite them, removing the qualifiers.

Take the Challenge: Exercise 33

Pick an aspect of your life (job, hobby, physical fitness program, etc) and begin to write the SOP for it. Start with the goal (What) you laid out for this way back in Tool One, in exercise 4.

Take the Challenge: Exercise 34

Write down a truth about yourself that you've never told anyone.

Now write down why you haven't told anyone. What are you afraid would happen if you did? How does that fear hold you back?

Take the Challenge: Exercise 35

Write down something you've done wrong in the past week.

Did you acknowledge the mistake to yourself? To anyone else?

Acknowledge it to someone else (especially the person you did the wrong to) and see what their reaction is?

Take the Challenge: Exercise 36

Pick a new goal from your list in WINS: Exercise 1. One you've yet to work with. Perhaps one that has changed, that you've refined, as you've worked through the later tools and areas.

Take the rest of the tools in order, and write a short summary of what needs to happen under each tool, just like I did in the Blood Lesson for the Q-Course.

This is your chance to pull together everything you've learned about how to become successful in your life. Review each tool as needed.

Take the Challenge: Exercise 37

Conduct an After-Action Review for your plan from Exercise 36. With your AAR done, incorporate all you've learned into a modified plan, then do it over again. Repeat as necessary until it achieves the change and goal you desire.

Take the Challenge: Exercise 38

Time to pull it all together. Fold a piece of paper in thirds. Label the left column MOE. In it, write down the answers to these questions—make them real:

While 'drinking' from the hydrant that is this book:

What stood out?

What angered you?

What made you afraid?

What motivated you?

What excited you?

What did you think was dumb?

What did you think was smart?

What did you think wouldn't work?

What do you think was something you could use right away?

What did you want to know more about?

Take the Challenge: Exercise 39

Your decisions. In the center column of the paper from exercise 38, label it Decisions, and write down what decision you want to make regarding your moments of enlightenment.

Take the Challenge: Exercise 40

Your sustained action. In the right column of the paper from exercise 39, label it Sustained Actions, and write down what sustained action you will have to do in order to change.

APPENDIX C: IMMEDIATE ACTION DRILLS

WHAT: Immediate Action Drill

Write down each goal you want to achieve in one sentence.

Check the verb in each sentence and make sure it is a positive one and something *you* control.

Make sure the outcome of each goal is something that you can observe and know when you've achieved it.

Check all your goals for conflict.

WHY: Immediate Action Drill

Using your one-sentence goals, write down WHY you want to achieve each goal: ie I am doing this goal for this reason.

Examine your WHY for options on how you can achieve the goal.

Examine your WHY to set boundaries for your goal, so you don't go to extremes.

WHERE: Immediate Action Drill

Examine your environment and see who and what will aid you in achieving your WHAT and changing.

Figure out who and what are hindering you from achieving your WHAT and changing and take steps to get rid of those distractions or negate them.

Research your WHAT (goals) and WHY (intent).

CHARACTER: Immediate Action Drill

Character is your core personality, both positive and negative.

Study your actions to determine your character and true nature.

Work on possessing the character traits of successful people:

Open-mindedness; willingness to surrender when wrong; balancing desire & contentment; having patience and self-discipline; using an active imagination and setting goals.

Understand that emotion is more powerful than intellect.

Figure out your Character, both strengths and weaknesses, by profiling your habits and also by comparing yourself to character templates, such as the Myers-Briggs.

CHANGE: Immediate Action Drill

Understand and implement the three steps of change:

1. Have a moment of enlightenment.
2. Make a decision.

3. Implement sustained action.

COURAGE: Immediate Action Drill

Going back to character, look at the opposite character type of yours in the Myers-Briggs and see what you are afraid of doing, then force yourself to do that.

Find your Blind Spot by using the traits, needs flaws diagram.

Expand your Comfort Zone by repeatedly venturing into your Courage Zone.

Catastrophe plan the various aspects of your life, predicting what the worst case scenario would be, and then being ready to face it.

COMMUNICATE: Immediate Action Drill

The purpose of communication is to evoke a desired response.

Writing things down make them real and delineates responsibility.

Read and listen carefully to get the true message being communicated by others.

Do you have confidence in your Communication skills?

COMMAND: Immediate Action Drill

You are in Command of everything you say and do.

You must have honesty and integrity at part of your personal leadership traits.

COMPLETE: Immediate Action Drill

Integrate and align the previous eight tools.

Use the three rules of rule-breaking to break out of the mundane and become successful:

1. Know the rule.

2. Have a good reason for breaking the rule.

3. Take responsibility for breaking the rule.

APPENDIX D: THE TOOLS
AS APPLIED TO THIS BOOK

1. WHAT do I want to achieve?

-Primary Goal: I want to write a non-fiction book showing readers how to use Green Beret tactics and techniques to conquer fear and succeed.

-Subordinate goals and alignment (partial list):

-Break the entire concept down into easier to digest Tools. (This subordinate goal was developed after the first draft and readers found the entire Green Beret Guide concept overwhelming in its entirety).

-Break the Tools down into each of three areas.

-Use examples so readers can understand.

-Give exercises to readers can apply templates to their lives.

-Coordinate the book with seminars, keynotes and workshops (possible conflict here in that the book has to stand on its own without my presence as a speaker).

-Market the book.

-Redesign web site to support the book.

(there are many more subordinate goals, but this gives you an idea of how primary and subordinate goals work—

and also how you have to look for present or potential conflict).

2. WHY do I want to achieve my goal?

-I want to write the Green Beret Guide because I believe the tactics and techniques of Special Forces can be applied to all individuals and make their lives better.

-Instead of throwing the entire concept at readers first, I'll give it to them piece-meal, starting with the simplest area, WINS, and build on that.

-Instead of expecting readers to change their entire lives right away, I want to start small, in order to not over-whelm the reader and cause them to quit.

3. WHERE do I want to achieve my goal?

-I am writing this book under the time constraints of also producing two novels, so I have to factor that into my scheduling and make sure I make my deadlines.

-For book dissection, I looked at numerous self-help, psychology, economic, philosophical and historical books and examined their information and structure.

-For further research, I examined the many different paths to change and success that experts propose and compared them against the proven formula we use in Special Forces.

-In the bookstore, there are numerous "self-help" books. However, most of them are either theoretical with few practical applications, or so focused they ignore the integration of all aspects of a person's life.

-In the larger environmental picture, this book is coming at the right time: the economy is in bad straits, there have been several large natural disasters, the country is at war, and people are feeling less confident than ever. This book fills a need.

4. Understand your CHARACTER and that of others.

-Profiling my habits, I discovered that I tend to do too much; to put too much information out there. In editing this book, I have constantly been cutting away material to try to focus the program as much as possible.

-I am an INFJ (author) according to the Myers-Briggs. Looking at the opposite character type to that, the ESTP (promoter), I realize I am weak in my ability to market this book and the Green Beret Guide program. I need to work with others who have experience in marketing and sales to compensate for this weakness. I also need to get out of my Comfort Zone and into my Courage Zone in this area.

5. What is CHANGE and how do you do it?

-The original draft of this book was 116,000 words. What you're reading is about 45,000. Remember earlier when I said one of the character traits I figured out was I tended to put too much information out? I changed. I cut and I cut and I cut to make this as straight-forward as possible.

-I focused on individual improvement and team-building when I first wrote this book. It got to a point where I was going in two directions at once. I had a moment of enlightenment and realized it would be confusing. Discussing it with my literary agent and getting other's input, I made a decision to focus the first book in this series on the individual. This was also based on the reality that individuals are the building blocks of teams. I then spent a considerable amount of time rewriting and rewriting what I had to achieve that goal.

6. How do you build COURAGE to change?

-This book is an example of catastrophe planning as it a parallel to my fiction writing career. The reality is that fiction is fickle market. I began the Green Beret Guide as a back-up plan to my fiction writing and because I enjoy teaching.

7. Communicate your change to the world.

-You're holding it. In the written form.

-I also do keynotes, workshops, consulting and seminars based on WDW where I combine this written form with oral communication.

-I constantly re-evaluate and adjust these based on feedback from the audience and readers.

8. Take Command of your change.

-I am responsible for everything in this book.

-While others are assisting me in marketing this book, the ultimate responsibility for it lies with me.

9. Complete the Circle of Success and change.

-This book is about Conquering Fear and Succeeding. This requires integration of many different aspects in a person's life. I've broken it down into three areas, with three tools in each. Laid out a step by step plan and then pulled it all together with the Circle of Success and by showing you entire plan laid out in Appendix A.

-This book breaks some of the rules for the traditional book in this genre. It's covers more ground and is more complex than most. I think that's important and made that decision consciously because I wanted to present a complete plan for all aspects of a person's life, not just one specialized area standing alone. I take responsibility for the success or failure of that approach.

APPENDIX E: BUILDING
THE WINNING A-TEAM

A winning team is built with confident, successful individuals. So this book is the first step in building a successful team. In essence what you do to build a winning A-Team is take all the tools in this book that are oriented inward, toward the individual, and turn them outward, toward the team. Below is a brief summary of how I help organizations build winning teams based on the most successful team in the world: The Special Forces A-Team.

When you walk around Ft. Bragg, you can tell who Special Forces are from a distance, even before seeing their Green Berets or their patches. They stand out. They exude an air of confidence.

Why are they confident? The training, yes. No other soldier in the army prepares in training like SF soldiers. And what makes Special Forces soldiers and teams so confident when they go on a mission? It's also the preparation. No other unit in the army prepares like a Special Forces team for a mission. So on two levels—overall, and specific mission, it is the *preparation* that is the key.

So the core of my approach for teams/organizations is this:

Cover in detail the flow of preparation that Special Forces utilizes. It's not about the mission itself when I apply it to the civilian world because the people I'm talking to are the experts at their mission, whether it be sales, IT, a sports team, educators, etc. But where I can help is show them the Special Forces way to prepare.

There is a specific flow:

1. Mission Tasking

WHAT: the goal is in one sentence with one action verb. On the back end, the clearly stated goals also equals the standard for evaluation.

2. The Commander's Intent

WHY: the goal is to be achieved. This allows for innovation and improves motivation.

3. Mission Concept briefing

COMMUNICATE: By the team back to the commander to insure the team is on target for the right mission and to explore options for mission accomplishment. Begins support planning. Rule out options that aren't feasible or can't be supported.

4. Isolation and Mission Planning

WHERE: If an Area Study is not already done, preparing one.

The importance of *Standing Operating Procedures* to codify actions, set standards, save time, and allow redundancy in the team.

The CARVER formula to analyze the problem and pick the best possible course of action.

COURAGE: Catastrophe and worst case planning to reduce anxiety and fear and allow team members to focus their energies on success.

5. <u>Rehearsals</u>

CHARACTER, COURAGE AND CHANGE: To insure priority of responsibilities and prepare for action.

6. <u>The Special Forces Briefback</u>

COMMUNICATE: To make sure all coordination through the organization is completed and ready. To insure all support is in place.

COMMAND: To get the Commander's approval for the mission or to be sent back to re-plan.

Then go complete the mission.

To make it interesting and exciting, I use a real mission my team conducted to show how each of these elements were used. I guarantee that even using part of this, either overall, or for specific tasks, will increase an organization/team's efficiency. So if any of you reading this is part of a team-- DARE YOU?

APPENDIX F: WELCOME TO THE WORLD OF SPECIAL OPERATORS

"Generally in battle, use the normal force to engage; use the extraordinary to win."
Sun Tzu: The Art of War.

When I took over command of my A-Team, I quickly learned that Green Berets were not the same type of soldier I had known in the Infantry. The Green Berets were not simply a 'better' version of the rest of the Army. They were a unit apart both in terms of individuals and organization. Throughout this book I will discuss the ways Special Operations Forces soldiers and units are different from regular soldiers and units and show you how you can apply these differences to yourself to make yourself and the organizations you are part of, elite.

What Can You Learn From Special Operations?

While you may feel your life is a far cry from that of a Special Operations Force soldier I do believe the concepts and tactics we taught at the JFK Special Warfare Center & School at Fort Bragg, and SEAL training at Coronado, and utilized in other Special Operations Forces are applicable to many fields. I used much of what I learned as a Green Beret in the artistic world of publishing and then as an entrepreneur building a successful business in under two years. I know many former Special Operators who are extremely successful in diverse fields throughout our society.

One of the first things I learned in Special Forces was that failure is not an option but you must plan for it in order to alleviate fear. I cover fear in more detail later in this book, but I believe it is the primary obstacle to success, even more so than lack of training or ability. My experiences in Special Forces showed me that people are capable of much more than they think they are. You would be surprised what you can do if you are focused on goal achievement and want it bad enough and are able to conquer your fears.

As an author I have learned that persistence is a more important asset than talent. In the entertainment business, which publishing is part of, many talented people give in to their fears and quit, while those with perhaps lesser artistic talent, but greater courage and persistance, eventually succeed.

The next thing I learned was that Special Forces (SF) are teachers more than fighters. One of the most common misconceptions about Green Berets is that their primary role is being a fighter. In reality, Special Forces was founded under the concept of being a force multiplier—of teaching others how to do the fighting. It was only because of their high degree of training that SF units have been drawn into other types of missions over the years.

During Special Forces training, a strong emphasis is placed on being able to pass on the skills learned to others. This ability makes for a very flexible and adaptable organization. Consider the investment you have made in your life in training (schooling and life experience) and the pay-off. Are you living in the best possible and most efficient way in order to achieve goal accomplishment?

A green beret is a hat that US Army Special Forces wear. It is also what Girl Scouts wear. A beret is perhaps the most useless of hats. It does not block rain well, nor does it shade the eyes, nor is it particularly warm in cold weather. Yet numerous books have been written about the 'green beret', movies made, and songs written. People have died trying to earn the right to wear one. A few years ago there was an article about a Special Forces student who was killed in North Carolina during a training exercise. The Special Forces Qualification Course class before mine had several students drown during a night parachute operation. During one class, students in Ranger School succumbed to hypothermia during winter in the Florida phase before rigid medical protocols were put into effect. Every person who spends any amount of time on a Special Forces A-Team damages their body in much the same way professional athletes are physically degraded, although Special Forces soldiers receive far less fiscal compensation for their troubles.

Green Berets are not what the media has portrayed them to be over the years. They are the quiet professionals. They are not Rambo's with a machinegun in one hand, a grenade in the other and a knife clenched between the teeth. We used to joke on my team about the knife used in the first Rambo movie. It might be good in a fight with a Roman gladiator, but it was pretty much worthless in modern warfare and a field environment. If you read David Morrell's excellent book, *First Blood*, on which the movie was based, you see how much of the original story was twisted and changed in movie development. In the following chapters I am going to try to dispel some of the myths that have arisen about Special Operations Forces so you have a clear picture of their world.

The core of Special Forces is the individual soldier.

These individuals are drawn together into the basic operating unit of Special Forces: The A-Team. An A-Team, is a highly trained, cohesive force that is capable of a multitude of divergent tasks, operating either independently or in concert with strategic level forces at any location around the world. During the Vietnam War, Special Forces soldiers were awarded a higher percentage of decorations than any unit before or since. In the recent conflict in Afghanistan, a few hundred Special Forces soldiers accomplished in a few months what hundreds of thousands of Russian troops couldn't do in a decade.

So enter the following chapters with an open mind. I'm going to give you a basic understanding of the world of Special Operations Forces and then delve into the history of Special Operations over the years. You'll notice I discuss failures as much as successes. There is a saying that those who do not learn from history are doomed to repeat it. That is the purpose of my series of books: *The Green Beret Guide to Seven Great Disasters*. To study the 'gift of failure' from the point of view I am putting forth in this book.

What you can learn from Special Operations Forces is a new way to approach life; a way that lifts you from ordinary to elite.

Who Are The Special Operations Forces And What Do They Do?

You've probably heard the terms: Green Beret; A-Team; Special Operations Forces; Delta Force; Rangers; SAS;

SEALs; Nightstalkers. You may have seen John Wayne and Sylvester Stallone portraying current or ex-Green Berets in movies. Maybe even read Robin Moore's classic book about Special Forces operations in Vietnam. Or more recently seen or read *Blackhawk Down*, by Mark Bowden, about Special Operations in Mogadishu. Or *Lone Survivor* about Navy SEALs in Afghanistan. *Twelve Strong* is one of the few movies that actually portrays Special Forces in a somewhat realistic manner. You've seen the headlines and watched the news reports from Afghanistan or other places, where a large amount of operations are conducted by Special Operations Forces including the killing of Osama Bin Laden by Seal Team Six.

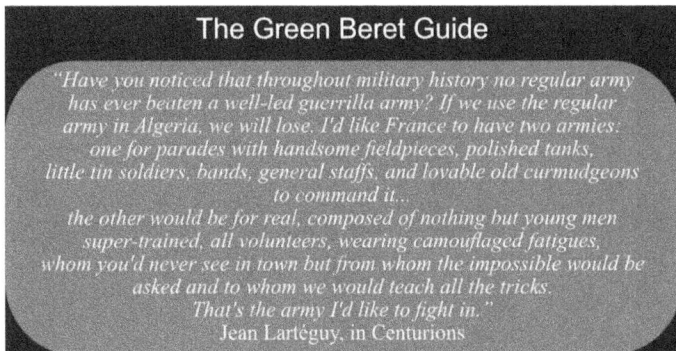

The Green Beret Guide

"Have you noticed that throughout military history no regular army has ever beaten a well-led guerrilla army? If we use the regular army in Algeria, we will lose. I'd like France to have two armies: one for parades with handsome fieldpieces, polished tanks, little tin soldiers, bands, general staffs, and lovable old curmudgeons to command it... the other would be for real, composed of nothing but young men super-trained, all volunteers, wearing camouflaged fatigues, whom you'd never see in town but from whom the impossible would be asked and to whom we would teach all the tricks. That's the army I'd like to fight in."
Jean Lartéguy, in Centurions

The French did lose in Algeria

Fact and fiction: Few people outside of the closed circle of Special Operations know exactly what Special Operations Forces do or how the men and women who are part of it are selected, trained and operate. (In some cases, we don't want you to know. There are certain operational aspects that must remain classified. In this book I reveal nothing that could damage our current Special Operations capability, nor do I discuss any classified information/events I was privy to or part of. However, none of those aspects are things that a civilian needs.)

I saw my first 'green beret' in person when I visited Fort Devens, MA, which at the time was the home of the 10th Special Forces Group (Airborne). I didn't need to see the beret or the shoulder patch to notice the difference in the people. Special Forces soldiers have a little bit extra of something special that is palpable even at a distance. It is the same thing you want others to feel when you walk into a room.

In order to understand today's Special Operations Forces we need to have a basic understanding of their lineage. This concept is also important in terms of yourself and your organization as you will see soon when we discuss goals. You have to know your own personal history in order to understand yourself. And you have to know what your organization was founded for in order to understand its structure and goals.

When I first became an A-Team leader in the 10th Special Forces Group (Airborne) my battalion commander gave me a book to read titled *Bodyguard of Lies* by Anthony Cave Brown. It's the history of covert operations during World War II. Reading about the deceptions, double-crosses, and bitter lessons learned at the cost of much blood and life, was an eye opening experience. It shaped the way I approached missions, particularly with regard to possibilities not inclusive in the mission briefing—something that in the civilian world is called 'thinking outside the box'. In combat operations the 'box', the situation envisioned with the best possible information, usually disappears very quickly once action is initiated. I was so enthralled with that book, based on a saying by Winston Churchill that I wrote a novel using the same title, about policing the world of covert operations.

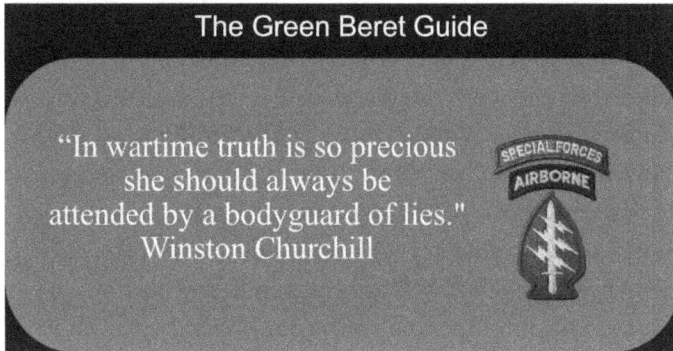

The Green Beret Guide

"In wartime truth is so precious she should always be attended by a bodyguard of lies." Winston Churchill

Being open to possibilities is a tenet of Special Forces planning and something I've found is essential to being an artist. If a person does something the same way as everyone else, then they are a craftsman. To create something different is the essence of an artist.

The Green Berets are the Army's primary Special Operations Forces—and the oldest-- and are called on to do a variety of missions which we will discuss shortly. I will break down both America's and some foreign Special Operations Forces in the next chapter in detail.

The Lineage of US Special Operations Forces

You briefly need to know where Special Forces came from. The reason for this is not to give you a history lesson (although there's nothing wrong with that), but to show how the five areas we're going to focus on were discovered, fine-tuned, and utilized. People died learning these lessons. While I hope your situation is not that extreme, lessons written in blood are the most poignant and enlightening.

Roger's Rangers

The first American Special Operations Force was Rogers' Rangers. Robert Rogers was a colonial farmer from New Hampshire who was recruited by the British in 1755 to serve in the French and Indian War. Over the course of the following years he formed a unit of colonials called Rogers' Rangers, the first Ranger unit. Unlike the Redcoat British, they wore green uniforms and utilized unconventional tactics, many of which were written down as Rogers' Ranging Rules, some of which are still used in the current US Army Ranger Handbook, as you'll see later when we discuss Standing Operating Procedures (SOPs).

The most significant engagement the Rangers fought was with the Abenaki Indians in Canada. This tribe had been raiding the colonies and was credited with over five hundred kills, mostly of civilians, during the war. A Ranger force of two hundred marched into Canada and destroyed the Abenaki village, a feat shown in the 1940 movie *Northwest Passage* starring Spencer Tracy. This was a case of thinking outside of the normal parameters on Rogers' part. Conventional wisdom at the time dictated being on the defensive along the frontier. Rogers realized that would be futile and leave the initiative in the hands of his enemies. The frontier was simply too large to be adequately defended with the scant forces he had.

He decided that the only way to stop this scourge was to go to the source, which others told him was impossible as it was too far inside enemy territory. He turned that thinking around, figuring that if the other side thought that too, it would increase his odds of success as no one would consider the raid a real possibility and be prepared to defend against it. This open-mindedness is something we will discuss shortly under Character as it is one of the seven character traits of the elite. An elite individual is someone who finds new ways to tackle problems.

The Rangers also fought in General Wolfe's campaign against Quebec and the subsequent one against Montreal in 1760. After the war, Rogers repeatedly petitioned the King to fund expeditions for the Rangers to explore from the Mississippi to the Pacific, almost fifty years before Lewis & Clark. Think how history might have changed if he had done this? Unfortunately, the King turned Rogers down and his persistence in trying to launch his own expeditions caused him to be arrested on charges of treason. So much for loyalty from top to bottom, a key to effective leadership, which we will also discuss. There are some who say the seeds of the Revolution were planted among the ranks of the Rangers because of this. Despite their excellent service, the Rangers were treated with contempt by the British and in 1775 some of the men who fired upon the British at Lexington and Concord were former Rangers.

Francis Marion—The Swamp Fox

During the Revolution, another chapter in the history of American Special Operations Forces was written, this time in the south. Francis Marion, another farmer, who was to become known by the moniker the 'Swamp Fox', lived on the Santee River in South Carolina. During the French and Indian War he served in two campaigns against the Cherokees. He was elected to the South Carolina Provincial Congress in 1775.

Marion helped fight off the British from taking Charleston for four years, before the regular army there surrendered. Instead of surrendering, he slipped away to form his own regiment which conducted guerilla warfare along the Peedee and Santee Rivers, defeating both Loyalist and British Regular forces, including Tarleton's dragoons. He was known for his hit and run tactics, particularly attacking at night and using the swampy terrain for cover and concealment. Like other Special Forces legends, Marion's adventures (somewhat fictionalized) were captured on film in the movie *The Patriot* with Mel Gibson.

A key to Marion's success was breaking the accepted 'rules' of warfare at the time. When Charleston was surrendered he was supposed to give himself up to captivity. He chose not to do that, much as some of the early architects of modern Special Forces, such as Colonel Volckmann, refused to give themselves up in the Philippines in the early days of

World War II and went into the jungle to form guerilla units. These were people who did not accept defeat in battle while the war still raged on. They were able to stay focused on the organizational goal and ignore the subunit tasking when it was not in alignment.

A dangerous, but useful tenet of Special Forces is to break rules when they don't fit either the situation or the mission. The breaking of rules is part of being an artist, of learning the craft and then rising above it. This is a core part of being elite. Later on, we will discuss the paradoxical three rules of rule breaking.

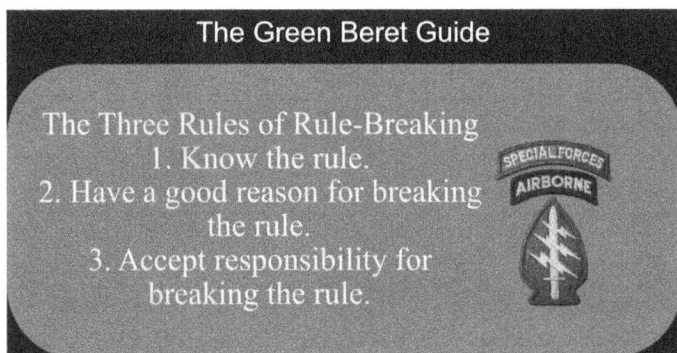

The Green Beret Guide

The Three Rules of Rule-Breaking
1. Know the rule.
2. Have a good reason for breaking the rule.
3. Accept responsibility for breaking the rule.

John Mosby

In the next major war on American soil, the third link in the history of Special Operations Forces was a man who fought against our government with great success. There are some Civil War historians who say that John S. Mosby's partisan activities in northern and western Virginia prevented the Union from winning the war in the summer of 1864.

Mosby wasn't a farmer. He was a lawyer who had a reputation for violence. When the Civil War started, he enlisted as a private in the 1st Virginia Cavalry. He received a field commission and worked his way up the ranks until he came into conflict with the unit commander and was reassigned to JEB Stuart's staff. He took part in Stuart's infamous ride around the Union army during the Peninsula campaign. Stuart then detached Mosby with the order to raise a band of guerilla fighters in the Loudoun Valley in northern Virginia.

With a small force of partisans, Mosby brought havoc to Union supply lines causing large amounts of Federal troops to be detailed from the frontlines to guard the rear. He ranged so far afield, he actually penetrated the outer perimeter of Washington's defenses several times.

In 1863 with only twenty-nine men, he stole into the Fairfax Court House and woke Union General Edwin H. Stoughton, capturing him. During another raid, he almost captured the train on which Ulysses S. Grant was traveling.

Mosby, like Rogers and Marion, used unconventional tactics to confound conventional commanders. His forces were always outnumbered and he usually operated behind enemy lines, taking the battle to his foe, rather than the other way around, as Rogers did in his march into Canada to stop the Indian raids. He usually lived off the land, much like we were taught to do during the Special Forces Qualification Course. Most conventional military units are tied to their supply lines which makes them predictable and vulnerable.

Mosby's forces so frustrated Union officers, that they took the severe step of summarily executing his men when they captured them. General George Custer, an example of leadership we'll discuss later, executed six of Mosby's men in 1864 and Mosby retaliated by shooting seven of Custer's soldiers. Mosby left a note pinned to one of the bodies stating that he would treat all future captives as prisoners of war as long as Custer did. Both sides ceased the executions, but an important lesson for all Special Operators is implicit in this. Often the normal rules of warfare are lost in Special Operations. If those outside of you break the rules to attack you, then consider why you are following all the rules that you do? Do they help you or hinder you?

Mosby's activities highlighted one of the keys of success for future Special Operators: small numbers of highly mobile forces can pin down much larger numbers of less mobile, regular forces and affect the strategic campaign well out of proportion to their size. Too often generals—and managers—are too focused on numbers of people and they ignore quality of personnel and the effectiveness of unconventional tactics. For the individual, the key point is that quality is better than quantity. Later in this book when we discuss George Patton, you will see that Mosby had a direct influence on Patton at the two met often while Patton was a child.

World War II

After the Civil War, it would be eighty years before the US military saw the need for Special Forces and much of the impetus came from across the ocean.

The Green Beret Guide

"Enterprises must be prepared, with specially trained troops of the hunter class, who can develop a reign of terror, leaving a trail of German corpses behind them."
Winston Churchill

Churchill spoke these words during the dark, early days of World War II when the Allies were on the defensive on all fronts.

The First Special Service Force was a joint American-Canadian commando unit activated on 20 July 1942 at Fort Harrison, Montana. The men were chosen for their outdoor backgrounds and the unit was initially slated to conduct behind the lines missions into Norway to destroy hydro-electric plants, or so they were told. One has to keep in mind subsequent commando raids on Norway's heavy water production—which were part of the Nazi nuclear weapon program. Sometimes things are not what they appear to be, another lesson elite soldiers have imprinted early in their career. As a novelist, I've learned that some of the best ways to develop plot is to take what appears to be one thing and make it another.

The Norway mission for the First Special Service Force was scrapped and instead they were shipped in the other direction to fight on American soil: at Kiska in the Aleutians.

Then, in an example of how flexible special operations forces need to be, they were shipped from Alaska to the mountains of Italy in 1943, a radically different environment. In their first action they took a German position in the mountains in two hours that had held off Allied divisions for weeks. After several more engagements, they were nick-named the *Die Schwartze Teuflen*—the Black Devils—by the Germans.

During the Anzio campaign, even though they were only at half strength, they held a quarter of the entire beach-head until the breakout, an example of force multiplying which is a cornerstone of Special Operations. They were the first unit into Rome and fought up the peninsula until near the end of the war when they were disbanded. Their exploits were displayed in a feature film, *The Devil's Brigade.*

A key lesson learned from this unit was the need to be flexible. To adapt to one's environment quickly, and to even adapt to a changing goal quickly. While we control what we do, we don't control the world around us. Therefore when the world changes, we have to accordingly shift to achieve our goals. When I saw that the future of publishing was shifting from print to digital, much faster than pundits were predicting, I made the daring decision to walk away from my lucrative traditional publishing career and build my own publishing house I went from selling 3 eBooks my first month to over a half a million in a year.

When we discuss the Area Study later, you will see one of the first things you must do is analyze the environment in which you live and work.

Several other 'special' units fought during World War II, including Darby's Rangers, the origin of our current Special Operations Rangers; the Alamo Scouts in the Pacific which never numbered more than seventy men, yet won forty-four Silver Stars while never losing a single man in combat; and Merrill's Marauders in Burma.

What all these units had in common was the philosophy of striking quick and deep behind enemy lines, leaving him confused and paralyzed. While some army documents say these units were the forerunners of Special Forces, they were more the prototype for our current Ranger Regiment, although their lessons were most certainly incorporated into Special Forces.

While the First Special Service Force might officially be the grandfather of modern Special Forces, in reality, most Green Berets look back to another World War II force—the

OSS, Office of Strategic Services, founded by Colonel 'Wild' Bill Donovan. Again, this was something that came from a British idea—the OSS was patterned after the British SOE —Special Operations Executive.

William Donovan is still the only man to have won our nation's four highest awards: the Medal of Honor, the Distinguished Service Cross, the Distinguished Service Medal and the National Security Medal. He earned the nation's highest combat award as a Lieutenant Colonel during the First World War. Returning to the States, he made a fortune as a lawyer on Wall Street. When war broke out again, he used his connections to convince President Roosevelt to form an American unit modeled on the British SOE.

The OSS was designed to operate behind enemy lines in small groups, primarily through linking up with partisan groups, particularly the French Resistance, although they operated in all theaters, such as Yugoslavia and Italy. In France, these small cells were called Jedburgh teams and usually consisted of an officer from each the Americans, British and Free French along with a radio operator.

In the Pacific theater, guerrilla units formed by men who disappeared into the jungle after the Philippines were overrun by the Japanese, formed the basis of covert units. Colonel Volckmann is credited with helping organize much of the resistance in the Philippines and developing quite a bit of the guerilla warfare doctrine US Special Forces utilized in its early years and still does today in the war against terrorism. I've read original After Action Reports (AARs) from Volckmann's units in the archives at the JFK Special Warfare Center & School at Fort Bragg. The lessons learned in them apply just as well to the present day and to places such as Iraq and Afghanistan.

In Burma, OSS Detachment 101 organized eleven thousand Kachin tribesmen into a fighting force that by war's end had killed over ten thousand Japanese while losing only two hundred and six of its own. This was made into a movie called *Never So Few* starring Frank Sinatra based on the excellent book of the same title.

One story about the OSS from the book *Bodyguard of Lies* that made a strong impression on me was about a Jedburgh team that was supposedly sent into a French Resistance network that the Allied commanders suspected had been compromised and taken over by the Gestapo. They believed this because of the messages they were getting back from the first team sent to work with that network. The way operators tapped out messages in Morse code was specific to each individual (their 'fist') and even though the code words the previous team was sending back were proper, they knew the person sending was not who he claimed to be.

Prior to departing, the second team was given a briefing containing information that was false, the team members believing of course, that the information was true. When they parachuted in and were picked up by the Gestapo, they were tortured and eventually gave up this information, which the Germans had to believe was indeed true. It didn't occur to the Germans that the English and American 'gentlemen' who ran the SOE and OSS would deliberately sacrifice a team of their own people like this. But as Churchill said: *"In war-time, truth is so precious that she always be attended by a bodyguard of lies."* And sometimes people have to pay the price to be that bodyguard. It was a clever scheme, if it happened, and very effective, except, of course, for the members of the sacrificial team. Makes you think doesn't it? More on this later.

At the end of World War II, the powers that be finally accepted there was a need for a covert operations unit at a strategic level. The CIA was formed out of the OSS in 1947. There were those in the Army though, who had served in the OSS, who felt the military needed a force that could work with indigenous populations either in a guerrilla or counter-guerilla mode and that the CIA was more focused on intelligence gathering rather than actual military operations (a turf battle that is still going on today).

As the chill of the Cold War descended on the world, the need for this type of force grew stronger. In 1952 Colonel Aaron Banks, a former OSS operative, convinced the army to form Special Forces to exploit resistance potential in Eastern Europe. This unit was to be trained on lessons learned in France, the Philippines, in Burma, and other theaters of operations. Thus in 1952, the first Special Forces unit consisting of a grand total of ten men was formed on Smoke Bomb Hill at Ft. Bragg, North Carolina.

APPENDIX G: THE RECENT HISTORY AND ORGANIZATION OF SPECIAL OPERATIONS FORCES

What have we done lately?

The first Special Forces Group formed was the 10th and it was oriented toward Eastern Europe as the Cold War enveloped the world. The reason is was labeled the 10th Special Forces Group (Airborne) was to fool the Russians into thinking there were at least nine others like it, thus even the unit designation was designed to deceive. Many of the early members were men from those occupied countries who joined the American army as a way to gain citizenship and in the hope of one day freeing their homes. The American Special Forces motto, *De Oppresso Liber*, came from these early days: to free the oppressed.

As the Cold War became hot in other places around the world through proxies, Special Forces changed its orientation to deal with this development. Among the first Americans in Vietnam were Special Forces advisers. They were there to train indigenous forces in counter-insurgency, the opposite of what they had been preparing for in the 10th Special Forces Group. It was a case of 'reverse thinking' something we will discuss later. The first official casualty of the Vietnam War was a Special Forces officer.

As Vietnam heated up, Special Forces began receiving more attention. In 1961 President Kennedy visited Fort Bragg. He inspected the famed 82nd Airborne Division and then the Special Forces. Impressed by what he saw and by what he had been hearing about Special Forces, the President sent a letter to the Army indicating his support for the previously unauthorized Green Beret, saying it was a:

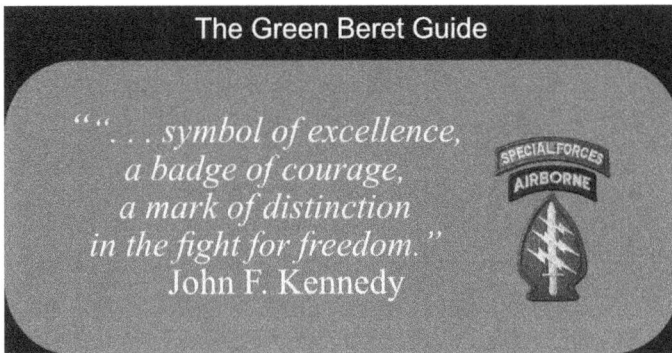

The Green Beret Guide

" ". . . symbol of excellence, a badge of courage, a mark of distinction in the fight for freedom. "
John F. Kennedy

Nowadays the two terms, Green Beret and Special Forces, have become interchangeable..

In addition to the Green Beret, there are two other distinctive emblems of Special Forces: the Patch and the Crest.

The patch: The arrowhead shape of the patch represents the craft and stealth of Native Americans, America's first warriors. The upturned dagger represents unconventional warfare missions. The three lightning bolts represent blinding speed and the three methods of infiltration– air, land and sea (if we get transporters, we'll probably add a fourth). The gold represents constancy and inspiration and the teal blue represents all the branch assignments from which SF is drawn. The Special Forces tab on the top was introduced in the early 1980s to distinguish those soldiers who had successfully completed the Special Forces Qualification Course.

The crest: The crossed arrows again link back to the Native Americans who were the original unconventional warriors on the North American continent. The fighting knife represents the character of the special operations solider: straight and true. Along the base is the motto of Special Forces: to free the oppressed. Crossed arrows also became branch insignia for Special Forces officers in 1987– I traded in my crossed rifles of the Infantry for crossed arrows when I was at Ft. Benning at the Infantry Officer Advanced Course, which made for an interesting time. One thing to remember about being elite is that those who are conventional often do not respect or like you.

Before we get into the most recent history of Special Forces, it might help to have a few definitions to understand the **World of Special Forces:**

Current Special Operations Forces

All elite units from all the military services consisting primarily of the following:

The Army

Special Forces: Will be covered in more detail later.

Rangers: The 75th Ranger Regiment consisting of three

battalions (approximately 800 men each). The Army's elite light infantry strike force. Capable of raids and short duration, intense missions.

Task Force 160, Special Operations Aviation Brigade: Also known as the Nightstalkers. Four battalions of helicopters. They fly three types, all modified for special operations: the MH-60 Nighthawk, a modified Blackhawk helicopter; the MH-53, a larger type of helicopter primarily used for carrying troops and supplies; and the MH-6, also known as a 'little bird' that can be both a gunship and carry a small number of men.

Delta Force was formed out of the Army, but now reports directly to the Department of Defense, not the Army. This is the military's elite counter-terrorist unit. It is stationed at Ft. Bragg, NC.

There are also Civil Affairs and Psychological Operations units assigned to Army Special Operations Command.

The Navy

SEALs, which stands for Sea, Air, Land. They are technically responsible for operations in water and up to the high water mark (although Osama Bin Laden was way above the high water mark). There are two SEAL Naval Special Warfare Groups (NSWG), one at Coronado, CA and the other at Little Creek, VA. SEAL Team Six is the Navy's elite counter-terrorist team. There are some other elements, Special Boat Units, that are considered special operations such as Swimmer Delivery Vehicle units.

The Air Force

The 1st Special Operations Wing, SOW, which fly special modified fixed and rotary wing aircraft.

There is also a Special Tactics Group and Combat Weather Squadron.

The Marines have formed the Marine Raiders, also known as Marine Reconnaissance Battalions, to be part of the Special Operations Forces community.

Inside of Army Special Forces there are five active duty Special Forces groups each consisting of three battalions with three companies in each with six A-teams in each company. The Groups each have a specific focus on different areas of the world. This allows them to become experts in those areas and also drives language training.

The A-Team

The A-Team is the operational element of Special Forces. It is designed to conduct operations completely on its own, unlike the rest of the army which has a hierarchy of tactical and strategic operations. The term A-Team is taken from Special Forces Operational Detachment Alpha, or SFODA, usually shortened to ODA, and then to A-Team. Its higher command is a B-Team, Operational Detachment Bravo, or ODB. This is the equivalent of a company. There are six A-teams per B-team. Above that is the C-Team, Operational Detachment Charlie, or ODC. This is the equivalent of a battalion. There are three B-teams, thus eightenn A-teams, in each Special Forces Battalion. Then there are three SF Battalions in a Special Forces Group. Got it? Right.

An A-Team consists of twelve men as follows:

Team Leader: A captain who exercises command of the detachment and can command/advise an indigenous combat force up to battalion level. Note that this fits is in alignment with Special Forces primary mission of being a force multiplier. A battalion of fifteen A-Team is capable of recruiting, organizing, training and fielding fifteen battalions of indigenous troops.

Team Sergeant: Officially known as the Operations Sergeant and the senior enlisted member of the detachment. He advises the team leader on operations and training matters. He provides tactical and technical guidance and professional support to detachment members. He prepares the operations and training portions of area studies, briefbacks and OPLANs, all of which we will discuss later. He can recruit, organize, train and supervise indigenous forces up to battalion size.

Executive Officer: Officially known as the detachment technician. Serves as second in command and ensures that the detachment commander's decisions and concepts are implemented. He prepares the administrative and logistical portions portions of area studies, briefbacks and OPLANs. This position is filled by a warrant officer. When I joined Special Forces this was filled by a First Lieutenant, but it changed shortly afterwards. I was one of the last of the First Lieutenants in Special Forces.

The Assistant Operations and Intelligence Sergeant: Plans, coordinates and directs the detachment's intelligence collections, analysis, production and dissemination. He also assists the Operations Sergeant and replaces him when needed.

Two Weapons Sergeants: Employ conventional and Unconventional Warfare (UW) tactics as tactical mission leaders. They train detachments members and indigenous personnel in the use of individual small arms, light crew-served weapons and anti-air and anti-armor weapons. They recruit, organize, train and advise or command indigenous combat forces up to company size.

Two Engineer Sergeants: Supervise, lead, plan, perform and instruct all aspects of combat engineering and light construction engineering. They construct and employ improvised munitions. They plan and perform sabotage operations. They recruit, organize, train and advise or command indigenous combat forces up to company size.

Two Medical Sergeants: Provide emergency, routine, and long-term medical care for detachment members and associated allied or indigenous personnel. They establish medical facilities to support detachment operations. They recruit, organize, train and advise or command indigenous combat forces up to company size.

Two Communications Sergeants: Install, operate, and maintain FM, AM, HF, VHF, UHF and SHF radio communications in voice, CW, and burst radio nets. They recruit, organize, train and advise or command indigenous combat forces up to company size.

The A-team is designed to be even more of a force multiplier when operating in split team mode, with one of each specialty on the two six man teams. Special Forces training will be covered in a later section of the book so I won't go into too much detail on each specialty.

Special Forces Missions

A Special Forces team is tasked to Plan and conduct Special Forces Missions as follows:

- Direction action. (raids, ambushes, demolitions, prisoner rescue, etc.)

- Reconnaissance. (the eyes and ears, usually at strategic level.)
- Unconventional Warfare. (Supporting guerilla forces, such as the Northern Alliance in Afghanistan).
- Foreign Internal Defense. (Supporting the government against guerilla forces, such as in Vietnam).
- SERE. Survival, evasion, resistance and escape. (Rescue those trapped behind enemy lines).
- Infiltrate and exfiltrate by air, sea and land. (We can get in and out of any place in the world).
- Conduct remote operations with little support.
- Train indigenous forces.

Foreign Special Operations Units

You might have heard of some of these units. As other countries join us in the war on terror, the Special Operations Forces of various countries have entered the battle.

The British Special Air Service (SAS) we'll touch on in more detail under Training. Their motto is: *Who Dares Wins.* The SAS in many ways was the lead unit in preparing to battle terrorism based on its experiences in Northern Ireland decades ago.

The SAS was formed in 1942 during the desert campaign in North Africa. Necessity is the mother of invention. The founder of the SAS was a Lieutenant named David Stirling. Their missions were usually long range assaults deep behind enemy lines. By 1944 there were five SAS regiments: 1 and 2 (British), 3 and 4 (French) and 5 (Belgian). When the war ended, there was almost a race to see which country could disband its SAS regiments the fastest.

Smarter minds prevailed though and the British SAS

was reconstituted into the 21st Special Air Service, interestingly also known as the 'Artists Rifles'. The number 21 came from combining the 1st and 2nd of the original regiments and reversing them—great minds think strangely on occasion.

With the 'Malayan Emergency' the SAS was brought back into combat. A unit called the Malayan Scouts was redesignated the 22nd SAS Regiment and gained a reputation as a top-notch unit. The SAS troopers were known to go into the jungle for long periods of time where they established close links with the aboriginal people—a tenet of Special Operations Forces. Other battles for the SAS followed in Oman, Borneo and Aden.

In 1969 the SAS began to get involved in operations in Northern Ireland where the Regiment started its hard-earned expertise at counter-terrorism operations. Most notable of these operations was in May 1980 when terrorists seized the London Iranian Embassy. The dramatic storming of the Embassy by the SAS was captured by the media and led to more publicity than any Special Operations unit prefers to have. It was also made into a movie. Since then the SAS has also fought in the Falklands and the two wars in the Middle East and in Afghanistan.

One of the best books written first-person about what it takes to go through Selection & Assessment and be in a Special Operations unit is *Bravo Two Zero* by Andy McNabb, an SAS member who was captured during the First Gulf War on a long range mission into Iraq.

The Germans have a unit of their border police called GSGG-9 to deal with terrorists. The Soviet Union had their Spetsnatz and it's interesting to note that unit's lack of success in Afghanistan against the successes of our Special Forces. The Spetsnatz was more a direct action unit while Special Forces allied with local forces.

Pretty much every country has an elite military force. There is always a place where those who want to be the best can strive to place themselves.

Now that you know a little bit about the world of Special Operations Forces let's discuss some relatively recent history, looking at lessons learned from both failures and successes.

APPENDIX H: THE
LESSONS OF HISTORY

While we all want to be original, the fact is that history does tend to repeat itself. When I teach novel writing, one of the steps I advise students to take before they begin writing their own book is to do a 'book dissection' of a novel that is similar to what they plan to write. This is not instructing them to practice plagiarism. Rather, it is telling them to study how someone successfully did what they are trying to do.

In the same way, there is no need for you to completely invent whatever it is you want to do in life. Others have most likely tried it and some of them have succeeded. Study the successes to see what to do. Also, study those who failed to see what to avoid. Learn from them. As you'll see when we talk about Character, I recommend not inventing your own template on personality types from scratch, but rather innovate from templates prepared by experts in the field.

Learning From Failure
"Don't do it this way," is sometimes as important a lesson as "Do it this way."

Many people and organizations refuse to look intently at their failures. There are numerous reasons for this. No one likes failure. No one likes making mistakes and most people particularly don't like admitting they are the one who made the mistake. However, not learning from failure makes the probability of the same mistake being made again very high.

I believe in this so strongly, I've written a series of books on it: *The Green Beret Guide to Seven Great Disasters: What Caused Them and How We Prevent Future Ones*.

As an author I've learned from my failures. I've had several lines of books and not all of them have been blazing successes. As a result, I began writing a book about how to write a good novel, *The Green Beret Craft Guide for Writers: The Novel Writers Toolkit*. I covered the entire process of writing a book. This is a form of writing a Standing Operating Procedure so that the same lessons don't have to be learned over and over again.

One shocking thing I experienced was the lack of information in publishing on how to be an author. The attitude was "learn on the job". I find that an inefficient way, especially when dealing with one's livelihood in a field where the odds of success are so low. I also still wonder if a large part of the reason the odds of succeeding at a writer are so low are because there isn't up front training and one is expected to learn on the job? So, I wrote a book about the publishing business from the author's perspective, putting in it all the lessons I learned the hard way. I found that the lack of institutional knowledge for authors is overwhelming and many new writers are quickly run over by the harsh realities of the business before they have time to learn the ins and outs and most important the reality of the business. *The Green Beret Business Guide for Authors: From Writer to Successful Author*.

If I had had the information I learned the hard way and put into the book at the beginning of my career, there is no doubt my career path would have gone differently and the time it took me to become successful would have been shortened considerably. I very much believe that I learned more from my mistakes and failures than I did from my successes because this type of learning requires change, something we will go into detail under people/character. Learning from personal successes does not require change, but rather continued success.

As you saw by the lineage of Special Forces, much experience was gained over the past two and half centuries by United States Special Operations Forces. More recently, Special Operations Forces have fought in numerous campaigns and conducted countless missions. Not all of them ended well. But it is only by looking at some of these failures do we learn lessons that we can apply for the future.

Vietnam

This was the first major action for modern Special Forces and historically the longest running. The first Green Berets in Vietnam deployed there in 1956 and on 21 October of that year the first casualty of what was to become a long list was an SF officer, Captain Harry G. Cramer. In September 1964 the 5th Special Forces Group set up head-quarters in Nha Trang and, until 1971, ran Special Forces operations in Vietnam.

Over two hundred and fifty outposts were established by Special Forces in Vietnam, most of them occupied by a single A-team fighting shoulder to shoulder with their indigenous forces. Over the course of the war, Special Forces soldiers earned seventeen Medals of Honor, ninety Distinguished Service Crosses, eight hundred and fourteen Silver Stars and over twenty-six hundred Purple Hearts. Given the low number of SF troops in-country at any time, this is the highest proportion of awards per man any unit has ever achieved.

But we lost the war.

While not getting into a deep discussion of the numerous factors for that, I will focus on Special Forces' role in the war and what was learned. On a tactical level, Special Forces were extremely successful. Whether it was the numerous camps established and held against overwhelming odds, or the indigenous forces raised as a force multiplier, or the covert teams sent into neighboring countries to gather intelligence, Special Forces accomplished the missions it was assigned. However, while they could do the subunit goals assigned, there was a lack of an overall organizational goal for the entire Army in Vietnam. This is something we will touch on in depth when we get to goals and goal alignment. It does subordinate units little good to successfully accomplish the missions and tasks assigned if the entire organization does not have a viable and defined goal. Sadly we've seen the same thing play out in Afghanistan. It does you no good to achieve day to day goals if they are not aligned with the overall goal you have set for your life.

Many lessons were learned by Special Forces soldiers in Vietnam. When I was commanding my A-Team in the 10th Special Forces Group, my team sergeant and I talked our company sergeant major into sharing with us the tactical lessons he had learned during his tours of combat duty. Many of them seem quite trivial, such as using paper tape on the pins of hand grenades to secure them from accidental release, but such trivial lessons were learned at the cost of lives.

Another key point here is that each of us is not the first person to face whatever it is that we are experiencing in life. Too many people and organizations try to invent something that has already been done. Learn from those who have walked the same path before you. Avoid their pitfalls.

After Vietnam, there were lean times for Special Forces. Three active duty groups were disbanded as the Army turned its attention back to Europe and conventional warfare. Special Forces troops became involved in a variety of activities including a program called SPARTAN, Special Proficiency at Rugged Training and Nation-building where soldiers worked with Native Americans building roads and medical facilities and in impoverished counties providing medical assistance. While noble in concept, this blunted the training edge as these tasks were done more to justify the unit's existence than to support the unit's mission. When we get to training, we will discuss making sure training is in alignment with unit goals, not as an activity in and of itself. This misdirection from training goals for Special Forces came to light in the next major operation.

In 1980, American covert units launched one of the most daring raids ever in an attempt to free the hostages in Iran. The newly formed Delta Force was the core of the assault force along with twelve members from Det-A, an undercover Special Forces Unit stationed in Berlin during the Cold War. Two members of my A-Team were part of those twelve.

The disaster at Desert One was well publicized. Many lessons were learned, particularly having units trained to do certain tasks and assigning them those tasks, rather than bowing to political pressure to piecemeal out the assignments. Task Force 160, the Nightstalkers, was created. A special operations aviation unit dedicated to those specific missions. I flew with the first Nightstalker units.

Contingency planning was also looked at, as the amount of slack in the original plan proved to be too little. When we discuss Isolation and Mission Preparation later, we'll get into this.

When I arrived in 10th Special Forces, the Group was in the process of conducting an operation in Lebanon trying to support a rather unclear national policy in that country. This culminated in the bombing of the Marine Corps barracks. The result was a withdrawal from a bad situation. Like Vietnam, the Lebanon mission was one that had vague and negative objectives. Your goals should not be negatives —they should be positive statements that lead to an achievable goal. You can't back your way into success.

The next major failure of Special Operations was in Mogadishu in 1993, which has been examined in both a bestselling book by Mark Bowden, *Blackhawk Down*, and a movie. Delta Force, the Rangers and Task Force 160 all participated. Tactical lessons learned—relearned-- were simple ones, some of which Rogers Rangers had codified over two hundred years ago. One was not to do the same plan more than once, proving the importance of knowing the mistakes and lessons of the past. More importantly though, the immediate pull out from Mogadishu set a dangerous precedent. One that Osama Bin Laden publicly declared he paid particular attention to, believing that Westerners had no willpower in the face of setbacks and casualties. This is a case where the immediate act had far-reaching, long-term effects. This is why a mission statement should not only include what is to be accomplished, but also why—the intent.

You should know not only what it is you want to achieve, but also *why* you want to achieve this goal. Because, as we will discuss later, sometimes the goal might have to change in the face of developing situations to keep to the more important intent.

In this vein, I want to finish the discussion of failures by backing up from Somalia, and talking about one Special Forces mission that has faded into history a bit: the Son Tay raid during the Vietnam War. The stated purpose of the raid was to go into North Vietnam and free American prisoners of war. Upon arriving at the camp, the raiders found no prisoners. Thus, the raid was apparently a failure. However thinking outside of the narrow perspective of the immediate objective, the raid achieved some unforeseen positive goals, something we always have to be open to.

The first and lasting effect it had was to build morale among the POWs. The fact that the government took a direct action to try to free them sustained many POWs through dark times ahead, letting them know that they had not been abandoned. Later in the book we will discuss Colonel Nick Rowe who was a POW in Vietnam for over five years.

There is a second possible effect of this raid, based on who you listen to. For a long time the United States had known that foreign advisers were working with the North Vietnamese in the relative safety of that country's borders. There are some I've talked to in the Special Operations Community from that time period who believe the raid accomplished a covert mission of killing a number of these foreign advisers at the camp.

From the failures of the past we in Special Forces

learned lessons that are incorporated into this book and from which you can also benefit. We also learned from our successes.

Learning from success.

Learning from success is a lot easier than learning from failure for quite a few reasons. One is that people enjoy discussing things that went well. Also, if something was a success, it is simply a matter of keeping up the same action, rather than having to change, although one must make sure the parameters are the same as that under which previous success was achieved.

While Vietnam was being fought, the rest of Special Forces weren't sitting idly by. Operations against guerillas in South America went largely unnoticed and it was only well after the fact that it was acknowledged that Special Forces played a large part in tracking down the Cuban revolutionary Che Guevara in the jungles of Bolivia. This was a case where Special Forces soldiers lent their expertise to indigenous forces to achieve a United States goal in a foreign country. In essence, they out-guerillaed, the guerilla.

During Operation Just Cause in Panama, Special Forces again showed its flexibility when a company from the 7th Special Forces group, code named Task Force Black, conducted a blocking action on a bridge across the Pacora River and despite being outnumbered by Panamanian Defense Forces, they successfully kept the PDF from crossing the bridge, inflicting large numbers of casualties while losing none themselves. What is curious about this was that the unit the Special Forces company was fighting was one it had just been training. The ability to quickly adjust to new mission taskings is a strength of Special Forces. They were also able to consider what capabilities the

Panamanian forces didn't have that they did, mainly night-fighting, and exploit this advantage.

During Desert Storm, Special Forces conducted a multitude of missions. Some teams trained Kuwaiti exile forces. Other teams went deep into Iraq on surveillance missions. Other teams were on station to recover downed pilots. General Schwarzkopf initially opposed extensive use of special operations forces. Only as the Scud missile threat grew greater and threatened to bring Israel into the war and destabilize the entire operation did he relent and give greater latitude to the use of Special Forces.

Between the two Gulf Wars, 5th Special Forces Group assigned some NCOs the job of figuring out a better way to hunt down Scud missiles. Note that you heard practically nothing about Scud missiles during the Second Gulf War as the 5th Group plan was implemented with precision. Additionally, when Turkey did not allow our large armor units to land in their country and be hauled to the Iraqi Border, it fell to Special Forces units to take on a task that armored divisions had been assigned. They conquered the northwest portion of Iraq by allying with the Kurdish people.

I was just doing some research and came across several articles written just after the events of 11 September 2001. There were interviews with former Soviet generals about fighting in Afghanistan and they were full of warnings about the potential 'bloodbath' if American forces went on the ground there.

They were wrong. Initially.

Afghanistan turned out to be the perfect Special Forces mission. Initially.

There was an indigenous force in place (the Northern Alliance) that could be contacted and worked with. The goal was clear and more importantly, was one every man could believe in given what had happened on September 11th.

While the Taliban regime was crushed, the subsequent nation-building has been marred by corruption, uncertain goals and a tribal and religious mindset that does not translate well to nationhood. It was not the initial goal. The politics of why we've attempted that are beyond the scope of this book.

Afghanistan and the war on terrorism has brought Special Operations Forces to the forefront of not only military, but geo-political operations. The world has changed. People and organizations need to change to keep up with it. Just as the Special Operations Forces have adapted to a new situation as proven by their success and failures in Afghanistan, so must you and learning how they operate will help you in this new world of the 21st Century.

Throughout all the failures and successes, it was the people who fought the battles who paid the price in blood. All the training, planning, conducting and critiquing of these events amount to nothing without the Special Forces soldiers who did them. Understanding yourself and others is the most important part of becoming elite.

APPENDIX I: LEADERSHIP STYLES

Another interesting fact that I was made to memorize as a plebe at West Point that struck me as quite odd that was that in 55 of 60 major battles of Civil War, West Pointers commanded both sides. In the other five, West Pointers commanded one side. In some strange way, the Military Academy was rather proud of that fact. It made me think that was why war lasted so long, which I don't think was the intent.

The other thing that struck me as strange was the number of West Pointers who fought for the Confederacy. While times were different then and state's rights were a much stronger issue, one does have to question a national military academy that lost a good percentage of its graduates to fight with a rebel force. Again, it all comes back to primary motivator. This whole matter interested me so much, I wrote *Duty, Honor, Country, A Novel of West Point & The Civil War* where I focused on the period between 1842 with US Grant and Sherman at the Military Academy, through the Mexican War and ending at the battle of Shiloh. This is the first book in a series that will continue on through the Civil War, examining the motivations and goals of both sides.

Now, we're going to cover several famous leaders and examine their leadership styles:

General Dwight D. Eisenhower: The Diplomat.

Eisenhower was a West Point graduate of the class of 1915, the class the stars fell on. Of 164 graduates, 59 became general officers, an amazing ratio of 36%. Omar Bradley was a member of this class. An interesting thing to note about Eisenhower is that he never personally saw combat. I would label Eisenhower's leadership style as that of the Diplomat, rather than General. He led the largest multinational military force ever assembled in history, even to this day.

Although he graduated before the end of World War I, Eisenhower's initial assignments were all state-side where he earned a reputation as a developer of training programs for the Infantry. He, along with most of his classmates, received rapid promotions because of the war-time environment and by 1920, he was a Major. However, like his classmates, the peacetime army was not kind to Eisenhower. He stayed at that rank for two decades. The 20s and 30s were lean times for the military and Eisenhower struggled to support his family. But he persevered while many others quit.

He had graduated 61st in his class of 164 at West Point, but Eisenhower improved his record the longer he stayed in the army. He graduated first in his Command & General Staff Course at Ft. Leavenworth, which garnered him attention in the small peace-time army between the wars. Looking at his career pattern, one can see that Eisenhower was more of a politician than front-line leader. In 1929 he toured Europe as an aide to General Pershing, producing a guidebook of World War I battlefields, not exactly a prime troop leadership assignment slot. In 1935 he joined Douglas MacArthur's staff in Washington and then followed MacArthur to the Philippines as his aide for three years.

As the army started to ramp up when Europe exploded in war, Eisenhower was finally promoted to Lieutenant Colonel. Three years later he would be a five star general. How did he get there?

One key was networking, which is important in any field. Because he had worked closely with both Pershing and MacArthur, two of the most influential officers in the military, he was chosen by Army Chief of Staff Marshall to head the Army's Operations Division just after the attack at Pearl Harbor. In this position, Eisenhower played a vital role in developing the strategic course of action for the military to pursue in World War II. It is interesting to note that the overall plan put forward by his division called for containment in the Pacific (which angered his former boss MacArthur) while prioritizing the defeat of the Nazis in Europe. One could easily make the argument this was more of a political than militarily sound decision. After all, the Japanese had actually attacked American forces and territory and there seemed little threat to the homeland from the Germans. However, Eisenhower saw the greater and more immediate threat to our European allies. He was able to see the big picture.

Because he was instrumental in making the plan, Marshall had Eisenhower promoted to Major General and sent to Great Britain to take charge of the American troops over there. In July, 1942, he was promoted to Lieutenant General and given command of the forces that were to take part in Operation Torch, the invasion of North Africa.

In his first overall combat command, Eisenhower's first

battle was a disaster. American forces were routed by Rommel's experienced Afrika Korps at the battle of Kasserine Pass. Not one to ignore failure or hide from reality, Eisenhower reacted vigorously to this setback. He relieved numerous subordinate commanders—some of whom had outranked him just months earlier. An excellent judge of character, Eisenhower replaced those who had failed with handpicked men who he had known during the long peacetime stretch between the wars.

One person who Eisenhower placed his trust in was a man we'll discuss shortly and whose style was diametrically the opposite: George S. Patton. Starting in North Africa, Eisenhower began the war-long task of dealing with two flamboyant subordinates: Patton and the British General Bernard Montgomery.

After North Africa, Eisenhower was in overall command of the invasion of Sicily and then into Italy. Afterward, he was brought back to England to take command of SHAEF: Supreme Headquarters Allied Expeditionary Force, to plan the assault onto the continent of Europe. A large part of his job was making sure the various nationalities could be brought together to fight as a coherent force. When you consider the landings in Normandy, you have to remember that there were five beach-heads: two American, two British and one Canadian, along with a large force of the Free French participating. The air, land and sea attacks were also coordinated with Resistance forces. While the coalition that participated in Desert Storm was impressive it was nothing compared to what Eisenhower put together in very little time. Also, an amphibious operation is the most difficult and dangerous of all military operations.

While Eisenhower never had to make decisions under fire, he made decisions that affected the course of history. It was his call alone to order the invasion to go in inclement weather on 6 June 1944 after a twenty-four weather delay, one of the most momentous decisions any person has ever had to make.

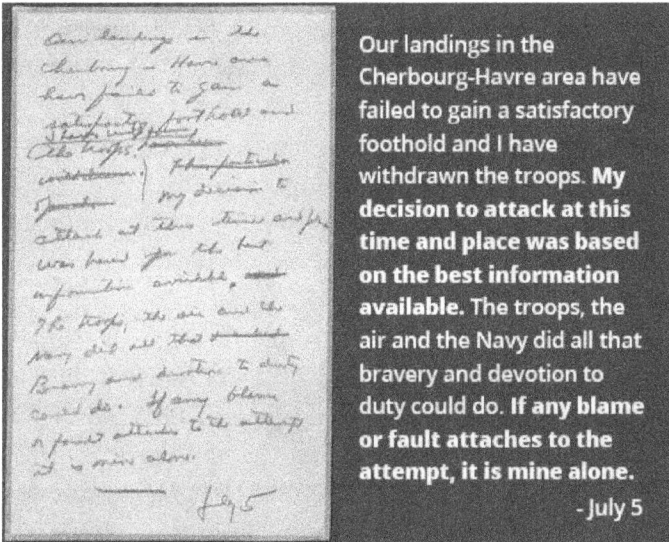

Our landings in the Cherbourg-Havre area have failed to gain a satisfactory foothold and I have withdrawn the troops. **My decision to attack at this time and place was based on the best information available.** The troops, the air and the Navy did all that bravery and devotion to duty could do. **If any blame or fault attaches to the attempt, it is mine alone.**
-July 5

Note Eisenhower prepared in case of failure.

From Normandy, Eisenhower managed the command of the Allied effort in Europe to the end of the war. Note I say managed—I think Eisenhower was more a facilitator type of leader. He brought people together and got them to work in harmony, allowing them to bring their best traits to the fore-front while trying to keep a lid on their bad traits. His use of Patton is an excellent example of giving latitude to a subor-dinate who had a particular talent. In the end, he had to relieve Patton because of political, not military, reasons.

Eisenhower's adeptness as a politician eventually led him to the White House, an office he won by the largest popular vote margin up to that time. He served two terms as President before retiring, curiously warning of the threat of the military-industrial complex as he did so.

Eisenhower's strength was forging and maintaining relationships among the Allies and strategic planning. While never having to prove his courage under fire, he proved it in his decision making. He was the right man for the right job at the right time.

General Douglas MacArthur

Douglas MacArthur was another West Point graduate, class of 1903. Unlike Eisenhower, though, MacArthur's career was steeped in controversy.

MacArthur came from a distinguished line of military officers. His father Arthur was a Medal of Honor winner in the Civil War. Douglas graduated top of his class at the Academy and was commissioned into the Corps of Engineers. It is interesting that while still a cadet MacArthur was called before a congressional panel investigating hazing at the Academy. Despite having been terribly hazed because of his family's reputation, MacArthur refused to snitch on other cadets—yet years later when he returned to the Academy as the Superintendent, one of his priorities was to reduce hazing. This indicates a strong awareness of his environment and how much he could affect it at different times, and how much it could affect him. A basic form of the Area Study as we discussed.

MacArthur's early assignments took him to the opposite side of the world from Eisenhower (except for the few years Eisenhower spent on MacArthur's staff), to the area where MacArthur would spend most of his life and have a profound effect on in many ways: the Pacific. He spent time in the Philippines and Japan, and accompanied his father, now a major general, on an observation tour of the Russo-Japanese War.

MacArthur returned to the States and served briefly as military aide to President Theodore Roosevelt. Later, he accompanied the punitive expedition that occupied Vera Cruz, Mexico in 1914.

In 1916, MacArthur joined the War Department and impressed many with his plans for integrating the National Guard units to fight with the regular army. When war was declared he formed a division made up of the National Guard units of many states (the Rainbow Division). He soon commanded a brigade in the unit and by the end of the war was the youngest division commander in the army.

MacArthur held a personal belief that the enemy could not harm him, an interesting concept to say the least. It allowed him, however, to lead from the front. While he earned a reputation in World War II as 'Dugout Doug' that was not the way he led in World War I. He ordered his troops to 'advance with audacity' and was always in the lead. He would go over the top armed only with a riding crop, wearing no helmet and not carrying a gas mask. His courage earned him four Silver Stars by the war's end and led Pershing to call him the "greatest leader of troops we have."

MacArthur remained on occupation duty until 1919 when he was recalled to the States to become Superintendent of his alma mater, West Point. At only 39 years old, he was, and still is, the youngest man ever to serve in that position. After World War I, given the horrors of the War to End All Wars, there was a strong anti-military backlash and the Academy was seen as archaic and out of touch with the time. The mark MacArthur left on the Academy was a large one and often over-looked by military historians. The Military Academy had changed little since the Civil War, and having personally seen what modern warfare was developing into, MacArthur knew the Academy had to change.

He modernized the curriculum (cavalry tactics were still in vogue despite the deployment of the machinegun and tank). He fought against the 'old grads' who wanted things to stay the same. Without his influence, our army leadership in World War II would have been less well prepared for modern combat.

From West Point he went to the Philippines for another tour of duty. Then in 1930 he came back to Washington to serve as Army Chief of Staff. Despite the fiscal restraints of the Depression, he fought to modernize the army, particularly the Air Corps and armored forces.

In 1935, he once more went back to the Philippines to help organize and train their military prior to independence from the United States. He retired in 1937 but remained in the islands with the rank of field marshal and as an adviser to the Philippine military.

As tensions increased in the Pacific, MacArthur was once more called to active duty by the United States and given command of US Army Forces in the Far East. MacArthur's personal feeling of invincibility must have grown over the years because he did not believe the Japanese were capable of not only hurting him, but of even attacking the Philippines. Despite nine hours of warning *after* the attack on Pearl Harbor, MacArthur still had not put his forces on alert. Thus the initial Japanese assault was able to destroy most of his air power on the ground. When the Japanese landed on December 22nd, they advanced rapidly against the unprepared American and Philippine forces. MacArthur and his men were forced back onto Bataan Peninsula.

At this point more controversy entered the picture as

MacArthur was ordered to evacuate the Philippines via a PT boat. Many have argued that MacArthur should have ignored this order and remained with his soldiers. On the flip side, his capture would have been a great propaganda coup for the Japanese and denied the United States his subsequent expertise in the war.

Here is MacArthur's CMOH citation:

MacArthur, Douglas
Rank and organization: General, U.S. Army, commanding U.S. Army Forces in the Far East. Place and date: Bataan Peninsula, Philippine Islands. Entered service at: Ashland, Wis. Birth: Little Rock, Ark. G.O. No.: 16, 1 April 1942. Citation: For conspicuous leadership in preparing the Philippine Islands to resist conquest, for gallantry and intrepidity above and beyond the call of duty in action against invading Japanese forces, and for the heroic conduct of defensive and offensive operations on the Bataan Peninsula. He mobilized, trained, and led an army which has received world acclaim for its gallant defense against a tremendous superiority of enemy forces in men and arms. His utter disregard of personal danger under heavy fire and aerial bombardment, his calm judgment in each crisis, inspired his troops, galvanized the spirit of resistance of the Filipino people, and confirmed the faith of the American people in their Armed Forces.

MacArthur escaped to Australia where he made his famous statement: "I came through and I shall return." Many found the CMOH award curious for an officer who had just abandoned his command. That MacArthur accepted the medal one can ascribe to his father's having won the same award, but it was still a low point in his career. Those who were left behind in the Philippines and would suffer the Death March and brutal imprisonment held few fond feelings for their former commander and his promise.

Because of the nature of the theater of operations, MacArthur was forced to share overall command with Admiral Nimitz. Surprisingly, the two head-strong men managed to coordinate their actions quite well. MacArthur's island hopping campaign was a brilliant strategic move and saved many American lives as they bypassed Japanese strongholds. Throughout the entire Pacific War, MacArthur lost fewer men than were killed in the Battle of Bulge alone. In the return to the Philippines, the Japanese lost 192,000 men to only 8,000 American casualties.

MacArthur was a master of the indirect strike. He did not like taking fortified positions head on. He preferred flanking to the enemy's rear and cutting off their supply and communication channels. Such a strategy was ideal for the Pacific Theater. Unlike Eisenhower, MacArthur did not particularly have to be a great politician as he held overall command and the Australians, Filipinos, and other allied forces gladly followed his lead. The Americans were the largest allied force in the theater anyway.

MacArthur personally accepted the surrender of the Japanese in Tokyo Bay on 2 September 1945. He remained in Japan and once more it was a case of the right person in the right place at the right time. He guided Japan on the course of economic recovery and into democracy with a deft hand. Having noted how revenge and retribution had had the wrong effect on Germany after the First World War, MacArthur sought to help the Japanese recover along a democratic model after the Second World War and ignored cries for revenge.

Unlike Eisenhower, though, MacArthur suffered from

hubris. While this worked well leading his troops into combat as a brigade commander in World War I, the higher he rose in rank and the further he got from his troops, the more this impaired his reputation. Some soldiers who served under him called him 'Dugout Doug' in World War II which is strange considering he had won four Silver Stars for courage under fire in the First World War.

MacArthur's hubris brought him to a crashing fall and derailed his own attempt at the Presidency during the Korean War. First, despite intelligence indicating what was going to happen, MacArthur as Far East Commander, was taken by complete surprise when the North Koreans invaded the South. While he wasn't good at anticipating attack, MacArthur was superb at reacting. As the North Koreans poured south, MacArthur decided on a daring course of action, going against the advice of almost everyone. The flank landing at Inchon proved an unqualified success and as he had done with his island-hopping campaign, MacArthur cut the North Korean supply and communication lines.

The North Koreans were forced to retreat in a rout and MacArthur led United Nations forces into the north. Once more, though, his pride blinded him to the larger picture. Ignoring orders and what his own intelligence was telling him, he pressed forward, crossing the Yalu River. This brought on a furious assault by Chinese forces and threw the Americans and their allies into retreat.

MacArthur was still in the age of total warfare and recommended that the United States bomb mainland China, and use nuclear weapons. His requests were denied and when he pressed the issue, Truman was forced to relieve him of command on 11 April 1951.

Despite being relieved, MacArthur returned home a

hero. The parade for him in New York City had an estimated seven million people lining the way. Congress invited him to address a joint session where he spoke his famous line: "Old soldiers never die, they just fade away."

As a plebe at West Point, I had to memorize another famous speech MacArthur gave: "Duty, honor, country." He gave it in the mess hall to the Corps of Cadets on 12 May 1962 upon acceptance of the Thayer Award. Some excerpts from this speech are of interest as they apply to things covered in this book.

"Duty, Honor, Country" — those three hallowed words reverently dictate what you want to be, what you can be, what you will be. They are your rallying point to build courage when courage seems to fail, to regain faith when there seems to be little cause for faith, to create hope when hope becomes forlorn."

One thing. As covered in the section under character, the elite person needs something on which to base their character:

"The unbelievers will say they are but words, but a slogan, but a flamboyant phrase. Every pedant, every demagogue, every cynic, every hypocrite, every troublemaker, and, I am sorry to say, some others of an entirely different character, will try to downgrade them even to the extent of mockery and ridicule.

"But these are some of the things they do. They build your basic **character***. They mold you for your future roles as the custodians of the nation's defense. They make you strong enough to know when you are weak, and brave enough to face yourself when you are afraid.*

"They teach you to be proud and unbending in honest failure, but humble and gentle in success; not to substitute words for

action; not to seek the path of comfort, but to face the stress and spur of difficulty and challenge; to learn to stand up in the storm, but to have compassion on those who fall; to master yourself before you seek to master others; to have a heart that is clean, a goal that is high; to learn to laugh, yet never forget how to weep; to reach into the future, yet never neglect the past; to be serious, yet never take yourself too seriously; to be modest so that you will remember the simplicity of true greatness, the open mind of true wisdom, the meekness of true strength.

"They give you a temper of the will, a quality of the imagination, a vigor of the emotions, a freshness of the deep springs of life, a temperamental predominance of courage over timidity, an appetite for adventure over love of ease.

"They create in your heart the sense of wonder, the unfailing hope of what next, and the joy and inspiration of life.

"The code which those words perpetuate embraces the highest moral law and will stand the test of any ethics or philosophies ever promoted for the uplift of mankind. Its requirements are for the things that are right, and its restraints are from the things that are wrong. The soldier, above all other men, is required to practice the greatest act of religious training: sacrifice.

"However hard the incidents of war may be, the soldier who is called upon to offer and to give his life for his country is the noblest development of mankind.

"And through all this welter of change and development your mission remains fixed, determined, inviolable. It is to win our wars. Everything else in your professional career is but corollary to this vital dedication. All other public purposes, all other public projects, all other public needs, great or small, will find others for their accomplishment; but you are the ones who are trained to

fight. Yours is the profession of arms, the will to win, the sure knowledge that in war there is no substitute for victory, that if you lose, the Nation will be destroyed, that the very obsession of your public service must be Duty, Honor, Country.

"The Long Gray Line has never failed us. Were you to do so, a million ghosts in olive drab, in brown khaki, in blue and gray, would rise from their white crosses, thundering those magic words: Duty, Honor, Country.

"This does not mean that you are warmongers. On the contrary, the soldier above all other people prays for peace, for he must suffer and bear the deepest wounds and scars of war. But always in our ears ring the ominous words of Plato, that wisest of all philosophers: 'Only the dead have seen the end of war.'"

MacArthur is one of the most controversial and interesting military officers in American history. As you can see from his life, he was a man of contradictions. Brilliant most of the time, incredibly blind to reality at others. Despite the nobleness of his speeches, he was one of the few American military officers to directly challenge the authority of his civilian commander in chief.

However, his Duty, Honor, Country speech summarizes much of what this book is about. They are words to live by.

Now for a character of a completely different sort.

Lieutenant Colonel George Armstrong Custer

Note that I use Custer's final rank, even though he preferred to use his Civil War rank of General. Custer is another of West Point's distinguished—or should we say—infamous graduates. He graduated last in the class of 1861, just in time to fight in the Battle of the First Bull Run, or First Manassas as it was called in the South (the South named battles after the closest town; the North after the closest creek or river, which often confuses people as the same battle has two different names depending on who you are reading or talking to).

By 1863 Custer was appointed a Brevet Brigadier General and took command of the 2d Brigade, 3rd Cavalry Division. He led that unit at Gettysburg and other battles. He won renown for his dashing courage, often leading his troops into battle from the very front. It is interesting to note that Custer's first command was a brigade, meaning he bypassed all the levels of subordinate command. His last command, the 7th Cavalry, was actually the smallest unit he was ever in charge of. It is also a little known fact that when Custer commanded the 3rd Cavalry Division, it had the highest casualty rate of any Union Division in the Civil War. Custer had a dozen horses shot out from under him, but was never wounded. Like MacArthur, this might have developed in him a blindness to his own vulnerability.

By the end of the war he held the rank of Major General of Volunteers in his mid-20s. With demobilization, Custer was forced back to his regular army rank of Captain, quite a demotion. He was eventually assigned to the 7th Cavalry, which he technically did not command, as there was a full colonel who held that title but did not take to the field, thus giving Custer practical command.

In 1867 Custer led the 7th Cavalry against the Plains Indians with little success. Bored, and perhaps lonely, without authorization, Custer left his command in the field and rode back to Fort Riley, Kansas to visit his wife. He was promptly placed under arrest for being AWOL. He was court-martialed and found guilty. His sentence was a one year suspension from the Army without pay. For a leader who demanded absolute obedience from his subordinates (to the point of ordering summary executions of soldiers for desertion, the same crime he committed), this is a rather amazing incident and very telling about Custer's character.

In 1868, Custer's court-martial was remitted and he rejoined the 7th Cavalry. Under the command of General Sheridan, a winter campaign was planned in order to catch the Native Americans in their winter camps. During this campaign, Custer's column attacked Chief Black Kettle's village on the Washita River, even though it was inside a designated Cheyenne Reservation. In this attack were sown many of the seeds of his later disaster.

First, Custer divided his command into four parts to try to encircle the village. Then he had all the dogs that accompanied the cavalry column muzzled and strangled to prevent them from barking and giving away the advance, even though he could have easily had the dogs leashed out of earshot, indicating a certain brutalness of character. Custer then led his men into the village and a massacre ensued—of the Native Americans.

At least those in the village. A patrol from Custer's command under the command of Major Elliot chased after some Cheyenne up the Washita and were caught in an ambush and wiped out. Custer refused to send aid after Elliot, instead withdrawing his command from the field as quickly as possible. This abandonment of his own soldiers earned Custer the enmity of many of the soldiers of the 7th Cavalry and also is one of those actions that Custer's superiors' should have paid attention to in order to evaluate his character and his ability to command.

As 1876 unfolded, Custer was once more in command of the 7th Cavalry operating out of Fort Lincoln in the Nebraska Territory. It was also the country's Centennial and a great celebration was planned in Philadelphia for the 4th of July.

Some feel that Custer's political aspirations were partly to blame for the events that would occur in June as Custer may have had a desire to present a great victory to the American public in time for the Centennial.

As one of General Terry's columns moving into the Dakota Territory, Custer and the 7th Cavalry moved toward the Little Big Horn River and a large Native American encampment. Afraid that his opponent would run, Custer made haste to attack, ignoring orders that he was to wait for the other columns to arrive.

In a replay of the Washita assault, Custer split his command into three battalions. He sent Captain Benteen, one of his most senior officers and someone with whom he had serious disagreements, along with three companies of men, off to the southwest, *away* from the objective. He sent Major Reno with three more companies to assault the village from the south. Custer himself took the remaining five companies of the 7th and rode north on the east side of the Little Big Horn to search for a way to assault across into the village. Excerpt from *Assault on Atlantis:*

Benteen and Custer were like two wolves prowling the same territory. Custer had the rank but Benteen had something else, a look in his eyes, which belied his gentle appearance. And the one time the two had come head to head, it had been Custer who had backed off.

Benteen was used to conflict, having grown up in a southern family that had owned slaves in Virginia and prior to the Civil War had moved to St. Louis in the border state of Missouri. When war came Benteen accepted a commission in the 10th Missouri, a move that stunned and angered his father who promptly disinherited him. The father went to work for the Confederacy aboard a supply steamboat that plowed the Mississippi. As fate would have it, the 10th Missouri captured that same steamboat, so the younger Benteen, disinherited though he might have been, held sway over father.

While his father was held in custody the rest of the war, Frederick Benteen served with bravery throughout numerous campaigns. He had been recommended for brevet brigadier general on June 6th, 1965, but the brevet wasn't approved due to the influence of politicians and the West Point network. Like many of the other officers now in the 7th Cavalry, at the end of the war his rank was reduced back to his regular army commission as a captain.

Benteen came to the 7th Cavalry in January of 1867. From the very first meeting he didn't hit it off with Custer. Benteen was older and he'd served more time with troops than Custer. But Custer was West Point and Benteen wasn't. Still, Benteen had tried to be professional. Then came Washita and the issue of Major Elliott that put acid in the moat between the two men.

The 'great victory' as Benteen would caption the event, had almost gotten Benteen killed. It was something he wasn't likely ever to forget. He'd charged into the village and spotted a young brave escaping, running from a lodge. Benteen gave chase, signaling for the brave to surrender. The man had turned and fired at Benteen, the bullet whistling by his ear. The brave fired again and the bullet hit Benteen's horse, knocking him to the ground. Benteen had rolled to his feet and finally shot back, killing the brave.

But it wasn't that incident that soured and sickened Benteen at the Washita. It began after that, when Custer ordered the Indian ponies captured by the regiment to be killed. Almost a thousand of the animals were slaughtered. Even here, under the harsh summer sun, Benteen still shivered when he thought of that cold December morning just before Christmas. He could clearly recollect the screams of wounded horses and Custer riding about, shooting the Indian dogs with his pistol as if it were the greatest sport in the world. Benteen shook his head as he watched Custer and Cooke talk.

Benteen jerked back on his horse's bit as he remembered. And then there was the counting in the village. Everything had to be counted. Bodies, saddles, rifles, spears shields, everything. Benteen had seen the official report and almost burst a vein in his forehead from anger. Custer reported 103 dead warriors. More like two dozen, Benteen had estimated from his own ride through the camp. The rest of the bodies were women, children and old men who couldn't even lift a spear any more.

And then there was Major Elliot and his eighteen men. Elliott had taken a platoon of men and charged after Indians fleeing down the river and simply disappeared. The rest of the command finished the butchering of the animals and the burning of lodges and then Custer ordered them to form to return to post. It would be dark soon, he explained to astonished junior officers who wanted to search for Elliott's party, and they had no idea if there might not be more large bands of hostiles in the area.

So they left without even looking for Elliott.

Benteen had been with the force that returned to the Washita two weeks later. They went downstream from the scorched site of the battle and found what remained of Elliott's command. Nineteen mutilated bodies lay frozen in the snow, inside a small hollow next to the river. Piles of spent cartridges next to the bodies pointed to a desperate last stand.

Maybe we could have saved Elliott, Benteen wondered not for the first time. If Custer had acted like any decent commander and-- Benteen spit. He'd played it out in his head a thousand different ways but the fact of the matter was that his friend Joel Elliott and eighteen troopers had been killed and torn apart while Custer and the rest of the regiment, Benteen among them, rode for the safety of their fort.

Benteen could still see Elliott's body, preserved by the cold weather. His arms had been ripped out of the sockets and placed alongside his head. Deep gashes ran down each thigh, cut through the muscle to expose white bone. His genitals had been severed and shoved into his mouth. The torso had been riddled with over fifty arrows. So many arrows that Benteen couldn't pull all of them out. He'd had to break them off to get the body into the burial wagon. Naturally, Elliott was scalped, the top of the head a mixture of white bone and red flesh.

Benteen wrote about the entire episode in a letter that he mailed to a colleague with whom he had served in the 10th Missouri. The letter found its way into the hands of a man working for the St. Louis Dispatch where it was published without the identity of the writer being revealed. It was a blemish on what Custer had claimed was a flawless victory and helped unleash a backlash of negative press, especially among the more liberal papers back east that decried the massacre of women and children.

Custer knew he wrote it. He threatened Benteen inside his command tent, a copy of the paper in his hand, and Benteen had asked him to step outside and take it up with weapons. Benteen had waited outside for more than a sufficient amount of time, and then walked away as Custer continued to rant and rave inside the tent but dared not show his head outside.

Benteen grimaced as Cooke and the new scout came up. The adjutant had his head so far up Custer's rear, Benteen often wondered if those damn whiskers tickled Custer's bottom. The scout was a strange creature, one of those who'd spent so much time on the frontier and alone, they didn't seem to fit in around other people.

Cooke relayed the orders for the march without meeting Benteen's eyes. Benteen didn't acknowledge the orders directly.

"Do I get a surgeon?" he asked.

"One has not been detailed to you, sir," Cooke replied.

"And if I make contact with the hostiles?"

"You are to pitch into them, sir," Cooke replied vaguely.

"'Pitch into'" Benteen repeated. "Is that a military term that is taught at the Academy? I am afraid I do not have the benefit of such an excellent education."

"You are to engage the enemy, sir."

"Engage with a hundred and twenty men?" Benteen asked rhetorically.

The adjutant rode back to Custer, whose back was turned to the column.

Benteen's military sense told him battle would be engaged today. There was too much evidence to ignore. And the battle would not be to the southwest, but somewhere along the Little Big Horn.

Benteen watched Custer for a few moments, then twisted in the saddle and barked orders, getting the three companies that were to form his battalion in line. He dispatched Lieutenant Gibson and ten men to form a forward screen in the difficult terrain to guard against ambush.

"Left oblique, march!" Benteen cried out. With a hundred and twenty men he began the march to the southwest.

"Where are you going?" Major Reno shouted from Benteen's left as the newly formed battalion began moving.

Benteen pointed. "To those hills."

"For what purpose?" Reno asked in a lower voice, coming closer so that Custer couldn't hear, although Benteen doubted the colonel could hear anything above the noise the column made moving.

"To drive everything before me," Benteen said sarcastically.

Reno turned and looked at the Wolf Mountains toward which Benteen's battalion was moving and his face reflected what Benteen felt. There was nothing more to be said. Benteen didn't particularly care for Reno either, and, if the truth be known, he'd rather have Custer in command than the major.

Almost immediately upon leaving Ash Creek the column hit rough going. That struck Benteen immediately in the tactical sense, telling him that no reasonable group of Indians would be camped here. They were down on the Little Big Horn as every sign and every scout in the Regiment had indicated.

Benteen smiled grimly to himself. The boy general wanted the valley for himself. Well, so be it. Custer and Reno could take on the Sioux. Benteen would do as he was ordered.

It's interesting to note the way Custer broke down his command. The officers of the 7th were a contentious group, half hating Custer, half worshipping the ground he walked, including his brother Tom who commanded C Troop. He also had a brother-in-law, his younger brother Boston, and his nephew Autie Reed with him. The companies that Custer took with him were commanded by those who believed in him, while those with whom he did want to share the upcoming glory were sent off away from the battle.

Having walked the battlefield and studied the accounts and history (including those from the survivors of the 'Last Stand', the native Americans), my theory is that Custer was one of the first casualties of the engagement. With his wounding, the element of the 7th Cavalry that was with him fell into disarray as his two brothers and other family members were more concerned with his welfare than that of the command. The five companies immediately begin retreating east from the village under heavy pursuit and the rest is well known history.

One thing that should be remembered is that only half the 7th Cavalry was massacred—not a single man survived from the five companies that were with Custer except the bugler sent with a message for Major Reno prior to the assault. Reno and Benteen's companies were surrounded and under siege for two days before the Sioux dispersed. The most Medal of Honors for any single campaign in US Army history—twenty-- were given to members of Reno and Benteen's commands, mostly for men who were willing to brave direct fire to crawl down to the Little Big Horn and bring water back for their wounded comrades.

Custer is an excellent example of poor leadership. He was the wrong man in the wrong place at the wrong time.

Colonel Joshua Chamberlain (excerpt from *Battle for Atlantis*)

Little Round Top. 2 July 1863: A wave of blue soldiers came rushing in from the east and raced up the hill and then partly down the western and southern sides, halting in a thin defensive line. This was the 20th Maine, under the command of Joshua Chamberlain, now the southern most end of the Union line, facing to the south in a curving line.

Fewer than five minutes after Chamberlain's troops arrived in position the Confederates from Big Round Top arrived at the base of the hill and began charging up the steep incline, weaving their way through the trees, undergrowth and boulders.

The men from Alabama ran right into the men of Maine. At stake was the entire fate of the Union army because if the Confederates could turn the 20th Maine, they would turn the flank of the Union army and accomplish what General Lee had set out in the morning to do.

The Confederates charged, to be met with close-range volley fire from the Union lines. The effect of the fifty caliber Mini-balls fired from the muzzle loaded rifles was devastating. Even a hit on an appendage caused so much trauma that many men died from such wounds. The screams of the wounded and dying mixed in with the rattle of musketry. The air around filled with gunpowder smoke, forming a man-made cloud that cut visibility down to less than a hundred yards.

Again and again the Confederates charged and again and again they were thrown back by Chamberlain's Regiment. Each time, though, like the incoming tide, the Rebels got closer and closer to the Union lines. The ground was littered with casualties, in some places so many, that the charging men had to run across the bodies of their comrades.

For those who have not been in combat, and even more so for those who have, it is hard to believe that men could stand such a carnage, yet the men in blue stood tall, firing steadily, and the men in gray kept coming. Another Confederate regiment joined the assault. The toll on the Union line began to show as the left flank slowly began to give ground, step by bloody step, back up the hill.

Soon the 20th Maine's line was so bent that it represented a V, with Chamberlain's position at the point, where he stood, issuing orders. Among the shouted commands and screams of the wounded, a new yell began to be heard—Union soldiers calling for ammunition. Over twenty thousand rounds had been fired and bandoliers were growing empty. Men stripped the dead of their ammunition, even darting forward and taking weapons from the Confederate bodies in front of their line.

The situation was reaching a critical point as the Rebel tide fell back once more, readying itself for another charge, the lines now less than thirty yards apart. Chamberlain gathered his company commanders around him and gave his orders quickly, trying to take advantage of the brief lull before they were attacked again. The shocked looks on the company commanders reflected the audacity of Chamberlain's plan. Despite their *surprise and misgivings, the officers obediently went back to their men and relayed the orders.*

Sunlight glinted off steel as the 20th Maine fixed bayonets. With a yell, and Chamberlain in the lead, the left branch of the V began to charge downhill, swinging in a pivot. In less than ten seconds they were into the startled Confederates who were hiding behind trees and rocks, gathering their strength and courage for the next charge.

Men finally broke. The Confederates had charged up hill, again and again, over the bodies of their comrades, into a withering fire, and they could take no more. The Rebel line broke and ran, the 20th Maine sweeping down among them.

A Confederate officer offered his sword to Chamberlain in surrender even as he pointed a pistol at the Union officer's head and pulled the trigger. The gun was empty and Chamberlain knocked it from his hand, sending him back with the detail that was gathering the prisoners.

Little Round Top was clear of Confederates and the Union left flank was secure.

Joshua Chamberlain was neither a West Point graduate nor a professional soldier. He was a graduate of Bowdoin College in Maine and spent three years studying at Bangor Theological Seminary, not exactly a hotbed for future army officers. He did not become a preacher, but rather a teacher of literature and writing.

When war broke out Chamberlain felt it was his duty to serve. Bowdoin was loath to lose him as a teacher and offered him a year's travel with pay to go to Europe to study languages. Chamberlain turned this down and offered his services to Maine's governor. He was made lieutenant colonel of the 20th Maine Volunteer Infantry Regiment.

Chamberlain saw almost all of the Civil War in the eastern theater, fighting in twenty-four major battles and numerous smaller skirmishes. He fought from Antietam through the surrender at Appomattox where he was chosen by Grant to receive Lee's formal surrender of weapons and colors.

The major reason Grant chose Chamberlain for this honor was his actions on the 2nd of July 1863, the second day of the Battle of Gettysburg. Chamberlain was awarded the Medal of Honor for what he did that day, a sharp contrast to MacArthur's Medal of Honor actions.

At the Battle of Petersburg, Chamberlain was seriously wounded when a Minie ball passed through his body from hip to hip. So convinced were the doctors that he was going to die that Grant 'posthumously' promoted him to Brigadier General and his obituary was written and submitted to the press.

Chamberlain not only survived, he returned to duty and fought through to the end of the war. When Grant gave him the honor of accepting the formal surrender of the Confederates at Appomattox on 12 April 1865, Chamberlain made the chivalrous gesture of having his men salute the defeated Confederates as they marched by, thus setting the groundwork for reconciliation between North and South.

After the war, instead of staying in the military like Custer, or going into finance or railroads as many other former generals did, Chamberlain returned to Maine and teaching. He eventually became President of Bowdoin.

Chamberlain did not view his time in the Civil War as a horrible experience, but rather a noble enterprise—a struggle of manhood involving courage, steadfastness and compassion. His religious background also came into play in that he saw combat as a place where one put their fate entirely into the hands of Providence. He had one thing, and unlike Custer, it wasn't himself.

Here is Chamberlains CMOH citation:

Chamberlain, Joshua l.

Rank and organization: Colonel, 20th Maine Infantry. Place and date: At Gettysburg, Pa., 2 July 1863. Entered service at: Brunswick, Maine. Born: 8 September 1828, Brewer Maine. Date of issue: 11 August 1893. Citation: Daring heroism and great tenacity in holding his position on the Little Round Top against repeated assaults, and carrying the advance position on the Great Round Top.

Notice that his citation is one sentence and to the point.

General George S. Patton

Patton was a person with a mission. As a child, he decided his goal in life was to be a hero. He drew this conclusion after listening to his father read to him the accounts of the famous Greek warriors from the Iliad, the Odyssey and other classics. Not only did he get a steady diet of the classics as a child, Patton often met veterans who came to his house. One of those who told Patton war stories we discussed earlier: a frequent visitor to the Patton household was John Mosby, who would regale the young Patton with stories of his Civil War combat experiences.

Patton had one thing driving him: he wanted to be a general officer and lead troops in combat. All else was secondary to him. It wasn't that easy though, as he had difficulty reading and didn't really learn until he was twelve years old. This put him behind the power curve in the step he had decided on after high school: attend the Military

Academy at West Point, an almost essential requirement to achieving the life's goal he had set out for himself.

Unfortunately, when he graduated from high school there were no appointments available to him in his home state. So he enrolled in his father's alma mater, the West Point of the South, Virginia Military Institute.

Patton spent 'rat' year at VMI and did well despite his problems with spelling, which would bother him the rest of his life. The next year he won an appointment to West Point and went from 'rat' year at VMI to Beast Barracks at West Point, which made for back to back very difficult years.

At the Academy, Patton was a dedicated athlete, in some cases too dedicated. His extreme aggressiveness, a character trait that would come shining through as a combat leader, earned him three broken noses and two broken arms while playing on the football team. He was also an expert fencer.

Despite his athletic exploits, his academic deficiencies caused him to be 'turned back' and he spent an extra year at the Academy before graduating in 1909 ranked 46th out of a class of 103. Note that he graduated six years before Eisenhower and Bradley, whom he would later serve under. He choose cavalry as his branch of service. He subsequently became one of the Army's best polo players.

Patton represented the United States at the 1912 Olympics in Stockholm in the Modern Pentathlon, which featured five skills that are basically military: riding, fencing, swimming, running and shooting. It is curious to note that Patton scored quite well at all the events except for shooting. It wasn't that he was a bad shot. On the contrary, he was quite expert with the handgun. However, while most of his competitors used the easily handled .22 caliber handgun, Patton felt he had to use a true military weapon, so he fired a .38 caliber. Because of the larger round, the holes he punched in the targets were bigger. In the last round of firing he was ruled to have missed the entire target, when in reality, his round most likely went through the grouping of holes he'd already put in the target.

In a case where examining someone's actions give you an idea of who they and how they act later, Patton, after the Olympics, was made the Army's Master of the Sword. He designed a new saber to be used by the cavalry, one that was better suited for the offensive than the defensive. He also wrote the manual to go along with the saber and in it he got rid of the parry—a defensive move—because he felt it made the user vulnerable to attack. Patton believed in being aggressive and always attacking. By now, you can see that examining these leader's early actions shows how they would act under crisis later in their careers.

When war broke out in Europe in 1914, in his desire to see combat, Patton asked permission to join the French cavalry. This request was denied as the United States was not yet involved in World War I. Instead, Patton joined General Pershing at Fort Bliss, Texas, where they conducted patrols and eventually went on the punitive expedition into Mexico against Pancho Villa. During the expedition, Patton personally killed General Cardenas, Villa's chief bodyguard, and another man using a Colt revolver. This revolver would later become his trademark, with two notches on the grip for his exploits.

When the United States finally entered World War I, Pershing brought Patton with him to England. Patton chafed being on staff and continuously asked Pershing for a combat assignment. Pershing finally relented and, since there was no US Cavalry on this new battlefield, Patton was sent to the newly formed tank crops. Patton was involved in the first major tank battle ever at Cambrai while with the British. He then attended the French tank course, after which he organized the American tank school in France.

At the battle of Saint-Mihiel, Patton led his tankers deep behind enemy lines, something he would perfect in World War II. He earned the Silver Star for this action. During the Meuse-Argonne Offensive, Patton was wounded by machinegun fire. He received a Purple Heart and Distinguished Service Medal, the nation's second highest combat award. While recuperating from his wounds, the war ended, something which must have saddened Patton while the rest of the world rejoiced.

Patton came back to the States and took over the entire Army Tank Corps, which sounds impressive but in the mid-war years wasn't much. It was so little, that the Tank Corps was shortly disbanded and tanks were given to the Infantry and Patton was reduced in rank to Captain, much like Custer after the Civil War.

Despite these roadblocks, Patton continued to lobby for an effective armor force and trained the men under his command ruthlessly. As the signs of impending war grew stronger, the powers that be finally relented and Patton was given command of an armored brigade, which would eventually become the 2nd Armored Division. By the time the United States entered World War II, Patton was a one star general. Remember, Eisenhower at this time was a lieutenant colonel working in the Plans Department.

In 1942, Patton led his unit in the invasion of North Africa. After the defeat at Kasserine Pass, Eisenhower, who had by now leap-frogged over Patton in rank and position, knew he needed a tough commander to restore morale and bring the attack to the Germans. He promoted Patton to

Lieutenant-General and gave him the 2nd Corps to command, the unit which had suffered the defeat. Patton enforced strict discipline on the unit and demanded that his officers lead from the front.

After successes in North Africa, Patton was given command of the 7th Army and ordered to prepare the invasion of Sicily. When the landing stalled, Patton went ashore and moved forward, joining a group of Rangers, helping push the breakout. Shortly after capturing Palermo, Patton was involved in the infamous slapping incident. Politicians in Washington and the American public cried for Patton's head. Eisenhower shielded his fighting general as much as he could from the criticism, knowing he would need Patton for the final assault in Europe. He put Patton on ice, so to speak, sending him first to Palermo, then Corsica, then to Cairo. The Germans carefully followed the movements of the General they feared the most They anticipated new assaults from these different locations even though Patton's command was hollow. By this maneuver, Eisenhower accomplished two things at the same time—kept Patton in his hip pocket and confused the Germans, an example of a 'tight' action, one that accomplished more than simply one thing.

Patton was finally sent to England to form the 3rd Army. While this unit was not part of the Overlord Plan (the invasion plan), it did serve a vital function in that the Germans believed it would serve an integral part in the invasion. This caused the Germans to divert attention from Normandy and, even after the landing started, to hold back reinforcements from the real invasion site as they waited for Patton's army to land elsewhere. The German General Staff had a hard time believing that the Allies most capable combat commander would not be involved in the invasion. For weeks after the landings, the Germans kept an eye locked on England, waiting for Patton and delaying reinforcements their commanders at the front desperately needed.

As the invasion began to bog down in the hedgerows of Northern France, Eisenhower knew it was time to turn his most powerful weapon loose. Patton, like a dog who hadn't been fed, was straining at the leash. On 28 July 1944, Eisenhower gave the order and the 3rd Army under Patton began attacking across Northern France, spearheaded by the 4th Armored Division.

Patton was turning Blitzkrieg against its originators. The 3rd Army moved so fast they by-passed entire German divisions, much like MacArthur would bypass strongholds in the Pacific. It is interesting that two of the most aggressive combat commanders the United States had in World War II, understood the concept of outflanking the enemy and avoiding frontal—and costly—direct assaults. Some say Patton and MacArthur cared little about their soldiers. Their nicknames in World War II were Blood & Guts and Dugout Doug. Some in the 3rd Army would say Patton's Blood & Guts meant his guts, their blood. But the numbers show something significant. Both commanders in the cold ratio of war, inflicted many times more casualties on the enemy than their forces received. Sometimes perception is not reality.

Unfortunately for Patton, and the Allied Army, logistical realities ground the 3rd Army advance to a halt. Running out of fuel and bullets, the 3rd Army assault came to a stop outside of Metz. Patton eventually took Metz and then the Germans assaulted in the Ardennes—exactly where they had used in their Blitzkrieg to destroy France so many years earlier. Someone was not paying attention to history.

When Eisenhower called his senior commanders to a

meeting to discuss what to do, while everyone else was pessimistic, it was Patton who turned things around with reverse thinking. His feeling was that the German assault could be turned into a great American victory if the Allied forces counter-attacked and cut off the German forces. Challenged to do what most considered impossible, Patton then engineered one of the great feats of modern warfare.

Patton disengaged elements of the 3rd Army, many of which were still in contact with the enemy, and led them north, into one of the worst winters Europe had experienced in many years. I served in the 10th Special Forces Group, which is the Special Operations Force that's considered the experts on Winter Warfare. I can tell you that everything is different when conducting military operations in the cold and snow. Every action requires careful planning and requires twice as much time. More injuries are usually incurred by the weather rather than the enemy. My first time at fourteen thousand feet in the mountains and at minus sixty temperature was an eye-opening and skin freezing experience. Every time we got ready to move out on our skis I would issue time warnings just like an airborne operation: One minute until departure. Thirty seconds. The men would begin stripping off their outer garments. By the time we moved, we would be in just our polypropylene undershirts, freezing, but a key to winter warfare is you do not want to sweat, because once you stop, sweat freezes on you.

Patton's success in the Battle of the Bulge is well documented. His prophecy that this could turn into a great Allied victory came true as hundreds of thousands of German troops surrendered. The 3rd Army did pause once more though, when it reached Buchenwald. Shocked and disgusted by what he found in the concentration camp,

Patton was the first Allied commander who instituted the policy of having local German civilians tour the camp to see first-hand what their Third Reich had done. He ripped through the veil of denial an entire country had been living behind for almost a decade.

By the war's end, Patton's 3rd Army had liberated almost one hundred thousand square miles of enemy territory and inflicted approximately 1.5 million casualties on the Germans. Staggering numbers by any standard of measure. But for Patton, peace meant his life's goal was complete. As the armistice was signed, Patton was beseeching Eisenhower for transfer to the Pacific theater. Ike, who knew both Patton and MacArthur intimately, naturally denied the request, knowing that throwing Patton into MacArthur's theater might cause more damage than the Japanese.

Patton was made military governor of Bavaria, which he wasn't suited for, but which Eisenhower thought would cause less damage than his presence in the Pacific. Patton got in trouble for using ex-Nazis in important positions in the post-war government there, but in reality this policy was probably a smart move as our failed occupation of Iraq demonstrated.

Patton also made his views of the Russians well known. He wanted to re-arm the Germans and make them allies in the war against the Russians. Again, Patton's foresight might have been correct given the following forty some odd years of Cold War that followed and the threat of nuclear war that hung over the world.

Patton, invaluable in war, was beginning to become a liability in peace. The problem was resolved when he was mortally injured in a traffic accident in December 1945 and passed away on the 21st of that month (which my novel *The Line*, takes a very different view of).

Despite his untimely death, Patton did achieve what he set out for in life. He was one the country's greatest combat commanders. Patton is an example of a person totally committed to their one thing and who achieved it and made his mark on history.

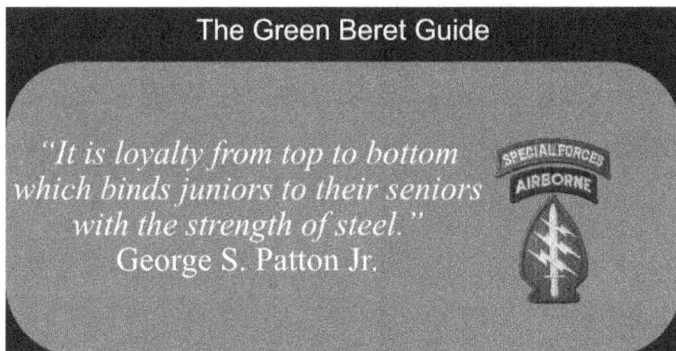

The Green Beret Guide

"It is loyalty from top to bottom which binds juniors to their seniors with the strength of steel."
George S. Patton Jr.

BLURBS

Chicken Soup Creator Jack Canfield:

"In the Green Beret Guide, Bob Mayer gives us a unique and valuable window into the shadowy world of our country's elite fighting forces and how you can apply many of the concepts and strategies they use for success in your own life and organization."

Lewis Merletti, former head of the Secret Service, Special Forces Veteran, and Cleveland Browns Executive VP and COO:

"Success in life- as in combat- has always demanded a depth of character. The Green Beret Guide reveals what it takes for you to move into the world of elite warriors and how their training developed that Can Do spirit and Special Forces ethos of excellence."

Commander 10th Special Forces Group:

"Demonstrates an innate leadership ability which sets him apart from his peers. He is particularly articulate with both the spoken and written word. Totally dedicated to mission accomplishment."

ABOUT THE AUTHOR

NY Times bestselling author Bob Mayer has had over 80 books published. He has sold over four million books, and is in demand as a team-building, life-changing, and leadership speaker and consultant for his The Green Beret Guide for Success concept, which he translated into Write It Forward: a holistic program teaching writers how to be authors.
He also consults on survival preparation and conducting Area Studies.

Bob has presented for over a thousand organizations both in the United States and internationally, including keynote presentations, all day workshops, and multi-day seminars. He has taught organizations ranging from Maui Writers, to Whidbey Island Writers, to San Diego State University, to the University of Georgia, to the Romance Writers of America National Convention, to Boston SWAT, the CIA, Fortune-500, the Royal Danish Navy Frogman Corps, Microsoft, Rotary, IT Teams in Silicon Valley and many others. He has also served as a Visiting Writer for NILA MFA program in Creative Writing. He has done interviews for the Wall Street Journal, Forbes, Sports Illustrated, PBS,

NPR, the Discovery Channel, the SyFy channel and local cable shows.

Thanks for the read!
If you enjoyed the book, please leave a review as they are very important.

Cool Gus Publishing
http://coolgus.com

✽ Formatted with Vellum

www.ingramcontent.com/pod-product-compliance
Lightning Source LLC
Chambersburg PA
CBHW050502210326
41521CB00011B/2293